A Chef on Ice

Sebastien JM Kuhn

Published by Seb, 2024.

A CHEF ON ICE

First edition. March 6, 2024.

Copyright © 2024 Sebastien JM Kuhn.

ISBN: 978-0648644057

Written by Sebastien JM Kuhn.

Whichaway

Neumayer

WFR
71°S - 8°E

SANAE IV

Mawson

Rothera
67°S - 68°W

Dixies
83°S

South Pole
90°S

Davis
68°S - 78°E

Casey

McMurdo
77°S - 166°E

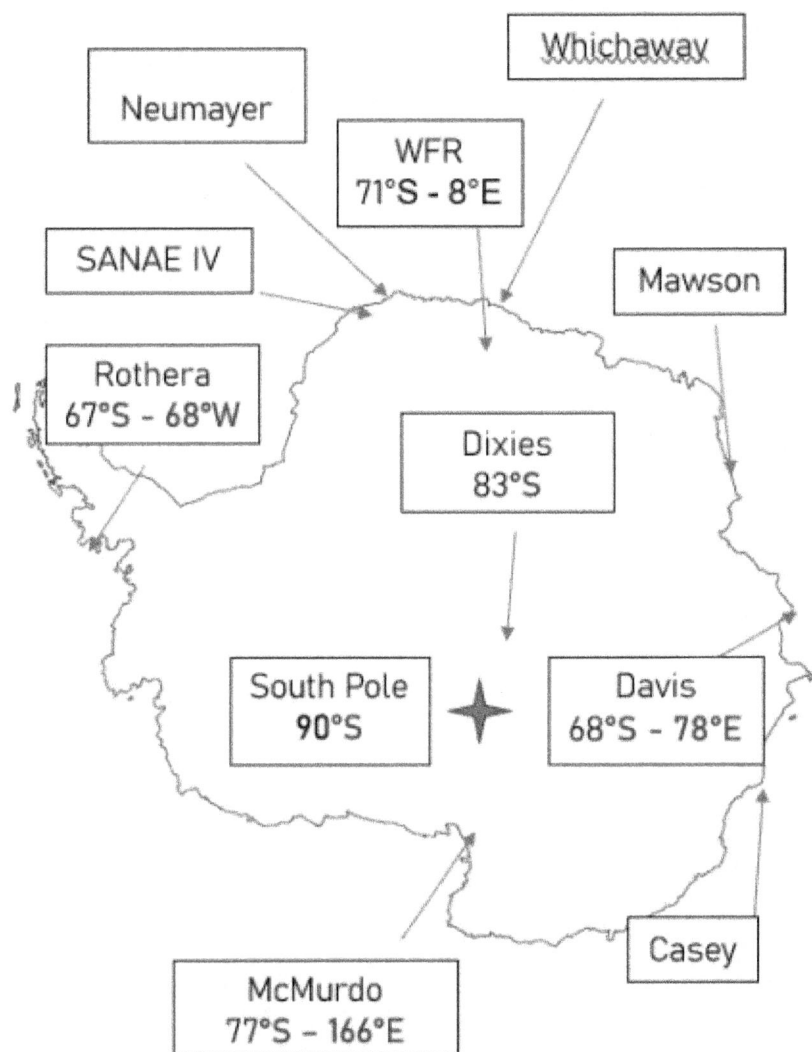

Warning: This masterpiece, created by Seb, is not meant for actual navigation to Antarctica. Please use a proper map if you intend on conquering the South Pole. Unless you want to end up stranded with penguins, then by all means, go ahead and follow this map.

Against all odds

Everybody needs a plan B. One tranquil Sunday morning in November 2013, I was in my house in Miami (Australia) working up the motivation to clean the windows. Mid-procrastination, I grabbed a newspaper lying on the coffee table to use as a cloth. When I flipped over the page, I noticed an advertisement written on the back:

Are you interested in working and living in Antarctica? We need chefs:
APPLY NOW!

I had always been drawn to far-off places, having spent months with the French Foreign Legion in Rwanda, Sudan, and Chad and later as a relief chef at remote mine sites throughout Australia and the Solomon Islands.

My immediate reaction was to jump at the opportunity; after all, Antarctica is one of the most secluded places on Earth. So, why not apply?

Without hesitation, I immediately ditched the window-washing project and jumped onto the Australian Antarctic Division (AAD) website.

My heart thumped with exhilaration as I scanned through the details and job description. Was this the perfect opportunity for me?

With my prior experience as a chef, I was sure that I had an excellent chance of being chosen for the position! I was overwhelmed when I began the recruitment process for the role.

The application requirements were daunting, with a seemingly endless list of qualifications that I needed to meet, both professionally and personally. Every part of me trembled as I collected all the necessary documents and evidence that showcased my abilities and competence. When I finally clicked 'send' on my online application, my heart felt like it was going to jump out of my chest with excitement.

Four months had passed, and I was finishing a contract in the goldfields of Western Australia, when I received an email saying that my application had been shortlisted and that I'd have to go to a selection centre in Hobart, Tasmania. I couldn't believe my eyes when I read the words that changed my life:

"You have been shortlisted."

The words themselves meant little to me at this point, materially speaking, but it meant the world to me that I had passed the initial application. I was thrilled to receive an invitation to attend a selection centre in Hobart, a place I had never been to before.

A month later, I arrived and met fifteen others like me who all wanted the same thing: a job in Antarctica, be it as a mechanic, a sparky, a plumber, or a comms operator.

We learned that three hundred of us had made the shortlist, and the AAD would be hosting twenty sessions over the next few weeks. It was then that it finally clicked that it was still a long shot of getting the job. But I knew better than ever that it was the chance of a lifetime!

At dawn on a Monday morning, I arrived at Hobart airport. The AAD representative greeted us warmly, and we were soon whisked away on a comfortable bus to the selection centre. After some time, we arrived at a hotel on the outskirts of Hobart, where we would stay for the next few days. Though it was stressful not knowing what was in store for us, I decided to adopt a positive outlook - after all, fortune favours the bold.

When we reached the hotel, we were told to label our luggage and leave it in the lobby. The concierge would take care of it for us so we could hurry to the conference room straight away, where a Human Resources team and a jury of six were waiting for us as part of the selection process.

Over the next two days, they arranged us into small groups and mixed us up so that everyone had the chance to meet and get to know each other. We went through a variety of hypothetical scenarios, during which we shared our opinions and reactions, either in a simulated Antarctic environment or in ordinary circumstances at home.

They instructed us to ignore the six judges observing us, which was much easier said than done, and just focus on being ourselves. There was no "right" or "wrong" attitude, but we were told to stay true to ourselves.

The day dragged on until late afternoon when we were informed that we would be taking a short break to go to our assigned rooms and freshen up. We would then reconvene for dinner in a couple of hours. To my shock, our rooms had been twinned with strangers, adding more stress to an already hectic day, but I chose to stay optimistic and relax. I made some quick small talk with my new roommate before taking a shower and changing clothes.

After getting ready, I headed outside for some fresh air, since we had been stuck inside the conference room all day long. I finally found myself in the dining hall with a small group of people. We were all waiting for dinner when a waiter appeared and informed us that the meal would be delayed at the request of our hosts. In the meantime, though, he announced that an open bar had been organised for us to enjoy. Not only was I famished, but I also craved an ice-cold drink.

As we approached the bar station, I noticed some hesitation amongst my fellow applicants. It was as if they were unsure of what to drink or how their actions would be perceived. But then I remembered the advice given earlier in the day: "Be yourself." So, I grabbed a beer without any qualms. To my surprise, it seemed to spark something in everyone else, and soon enough, they too were revelling in their drinks.

Eventually, our hosts showed up and dinner was served. This time, though, there was a twist: the meal was laid out like a buffet, but instead of tables inside, there were only a few high bar tables. The outside, however, had several tables and benches for us to sit at while eating. Everyone seemed a bit perplexed, unsure of whether to stay in and eat standing up with everyone else or take their food outside and enjoy it in comfort. I decided to follow my impulses, thinking that if I left the room, I would still have plenty of time afterward to socialise. To my surprise, others followed me, including a few from the judging panel. At that moment, I knew I was on the right track.

The night went on until past midnight, when one of our hosts informed us that we would have an early start the next day so we could finish up by the afternoon and make it back to the airport for our return flights home.

The next morning, I rose early, showered, packed, and made my way to the restaurant for breakfast. The atmosphere was much different from the night before, with everyone only having had a few hours of sleep. The day quickly blended into one long session with frenzied switching between groups. You could identify shifts in people's personalities as the tempo, pressure, and resulting exhaustion intensified. At the end of the day, the HR person running the selection centre declared that our last activity would be an around-the-table declaration of why we were worthy of being hired by AAD, and what we could bring to an Antarctic team.

My mind went blank: how would I impress them? It seemed that the moderator was picking individuals to answer the question in a specific order, with those who had contributed the least during the two days before being called first. This made me suspect that I might be among the last to be asked.

As I watched each person give their answer, all saying similar things with slight differences, I noticed the judges' attention drifting. It was clear they were looking for something different, something individual, something with a little "je ne sais quoi." I had to think fast - what could I do to make my response stand out?

Suddenly, I heard my name called out and I realised I was the last one left. Even though I had no idea of what to say, I began talking anyway. I stood up and said, "Cooking is a passion of mine- I love the feeling of preparing a delicious meal to be shared with family and friends. If you need someone to take care of your meals - whether it's for health reasons, or just to make sure you're being taken care of - then you need me on your team!" After I finished speaking, some people in the audience chuckled, so I quickly continued with my pitch about why the AAD should hire me as a chef in Antarctica.

I took care to mention that it would make me very, very, very happy to go to Antarctica, and by the time I was done, all of the judges were smiling. Still, I knew that whatever happened next was in their hands. Once I had finished, we were promptly ushered onto the shuttle to head back to the airport. It had been an exhausting few days, but as I settled into my seat, I was convinced that I had a realistic chance of getting the job. I knew that it may take time to hear back, though, so I tried to put my head back and relax. I needed to put it out of my mind and get on with the upcoming weeks and months.

As it happened, it was pretty easy to do just that. In all honesty, life was pretty great at that moment in time. I travelled around some amazing places, made decent money on remote mine sites, and even done a stint in the Solomon Islands with my own chauffeur taking me around.

All thoughts of Antarctica were soon forgotten, until yet another email came through requesting police clearance certificates, medical assessments, and psychological profiling. The recruitment process was unlike anything I had ever seen before - it felt like being on a TV show and waiting to see if I'd make it through to the next round.

It was 2 p.m. on a blistering day deep in Dysart, Queensland when my phone jarred me awake from what had been a brief respite in my sleep. I had been toiling through the night shift and desperately wanted rest.

On the other end of the line was the Human Resources department of the Australian Antarctic Division, inquiring if I still wanted to take them up on their offer of a chef position in Antarctica. My "yes" was instantaneous. After months and months of anticipation and readying myself, this felt like an out-of-body experience. This was the phone call I had been yearning for!

My mind raced with questions - what would living in Antarctica be like? Would I be able to survive in such a hostile environment? My anxiety was assuaged when I received further instructions and preparations for the trip, including details on insurance, equipment, and clothing.

Before I knew it, I was packing up my few possessions for a journey to a place to which none of my family or friends had ever been before.

I searched the Gold Coast fervently for gloves, socks, beanies, snow boots, goggles, and other winter wear that would fulfill my needs, but before spending a fortune, I decided I should wait until I arrived in Hobart to find a better selection.

At the same time, I planned a special sendoff party for myself. Invitations were sent out with instructions for guests to arrive in winter attire. I turned the air conditioner temperature down low with the fan setting on high, windows were blacked out, special fluoro-black lights were set up, two smoke machines were installed, and six bags of polystyrene beanbag filling were scattered across the floor. It was an astounding sight! We spent the day making snow angels on the lounge room floor amid a sweltering Australian summer's day with the temperature in the high 30s and 90% humidity.

Inside, for the evening feast, I had meticulously arranged a lavish spread of exquisite finger foods, such as thinly sliced beef carpaccio, zesty salmon tartare, and a variety of opulent dips and antipasto platters to leave everyone in awe. The final touch was a plentiful helping of velvety-smooth ice cream for dessert. To warm our cockles from the cold, I poured mulled wine into delicate crystal glasses - a little gesture to mirror the atmosphere outside the house. We dined in comfort among friends and had huge amounts of fun - so much so that I was still cleaning up the mess the next morning when the time came for me to leave and board my flight to Hobart. What a predicament! As if packing my bags wasn't already challenging enough, I'd gone and spilled all these polystyrene beans everywhere. They had proven even harder to deal with thanks to their pesky electrostatic conduction. I was still finding some of them scattered around long after returning from Antarctica.

The Aurora Australis

When I arrived in Hobart, I was introduced to the rest of the team that had gone on our mission to Antarctica. Our group comprised a diverse range of talents and backgrounds from all across Australia: carpenters, electricians, mechanics, plumbers, medical professionals, scientists, helicopter pilots, and aviation technicians, to name but a few.

We had undergone two weeks of arduous training in topics such as firefighting, extreme environment survival skills, search & rescue operations, first aid techniques, quad bike operations, communications procedures, and job-specific orientations for each individual (in my case, these were related to food & beverage). Even the carpenter was taught how to act as an assistant during surgery if needed. All of the necessary elements for our expedition had been arranged by our employer.

We knew that once we reached Antarctica, we would have to rely solely on ourselves for living and staying safe. I also got the chance to meet the person in charge of food and beverages, who had hired me for the role.

Most importantly though, we were provided with polar gear - thermal clothing, outer layers, snow boots - and survival bags which could help save us should anything go wrong in one of the most hostile habitats on Earth. It struck me then how fortunate I was to be partaking in this unique experience.

Before we set sail, a member of the Australian Antarctic Division held a meeting in which she gave us instructions about safety protocols that had to be followed while aboard or active on land during our stay in Antarctica.

Two days later, we set sail, full of enthusiasm., Though we were still a bit apprehensive at spending months in such a harsh environment, we were eager to see what Antarctica had in store for us.

Years ago, my friend Scott had given me a book called "Voyage for Mad Men" - a real-life account of the first-ever solo circumnavigation of the Earth. As I read about the race, I discovered that the tempestuous winds of the Roaring 40s, Furious 50s, and Screaming 60s mercilessly ravaged the Southern Ocean on the outskirts of Antarctica. These names were not given lightly, but rather as a warning to all who dared traverse these latitudes. Their ferocity certainly conjures up visions of terror and annihilation for me - and for good reason: these winds have long been dreaded for their ability to wreak utter devastation upon anything in their path. In fact, their very existence has dictated the treacherous paths taken by ships brave enough to sail through this nautical nightmare. As I read, I felt more and more thrilled to embark on my own adventures!

Standing on the wharf, I paused to look at the ship and suddenly recalled a phrase my grandmother's sister frequently said when I was growing up in France: "One day, on a nice day..." With that memory in mind, I thought to myself, "One day, on a nice day, I will go to Antarctica!" At last, that nice day had come.

The sun glimmered in the sky as we clambered aboard an icebreaker vessel, ready to embark on a journey across the sea that would take us to Antarctica within the next 10-15 days, depending on the weather and progress made while cutting through the solid pack ice.

We received our final safety briefing before setting off, once again giving us a clear reminder of what actions must be taken in case of an emergency. Suddenly, it dawned on me that the sinking of the Titanic wasn't all that long ago!

Fortunately, those musings soon evaporated as we left port and were just as swiftly replaced with pride, joy, and sheer excitement. After a few days of getting to know each other better, we all eventually started to become more comfortable and find our own space within the vessel.

Despite the cramped living quarters, we all managed to find ways to make ourselves at home. Each sleeping cabin had two bunk beds and an ensuite bathroom, with a small porthole from which you could behold passing icebergs or gaze upon the star-studded night sky.

The nights grew shorter and shorter as we sailed further south. Before too long, we were in the throes of summertime, with daylight lasting 24 hours a day. The days melded into one another as we ventured south, the sun never setting and casting a relentless glare around us. We were trapped in an endless summer with time losing all sense of structure under this blinding light.

Each moment felt like a twisted eternity, disorientating and surreal as we journeyed through this bizarre new world. We took some time to familiarise ourselves with the ship's safety procedures and our assigned roles on board.

I had the opportunity to assist the head chef in the galley as the young chef assisting him was on his maiden voyage and feeling ill, so he needed some rest. The heat of any professional kitchen, the pressure to work fast, and the constant need to meet meal deadlines made being a chef hard enough, but when you added in a constant fight for balance on a swaying, pitching ship, the job became even tougher. The kitchen buzzed with energy as we cut vegetables and stirred pots of sauce.

We moved swiftly around the stovetops, keeping one hand on the rail surrounding the kitchen and the other on the stove as the boat rocked back and forth, plates clinking against their shelves. Every moment spent in the kitchen was a fight, with the oppressive heat being exacerbated by continuous tension to act quickly enough to produce an ever-growing demand for meals to be ready on time. I tried to place sizzling steaks from the grill into a serving pan while managing to keep it steady despite the constant up and down of the boat.

The air was thick with steam and the wafting aromas of herbs roasting over blazing heat. Despite all these challenging conditions, though, we somehow managed to present impressive dishes that made everyone who could make it to the dining room happy. I have often referred to the experience as the perfect storm in the galley! It was incredible to contribute something meaningful to the journey. I was worried about getting seasick, but in the end, I felt fine; if anything, I was more ravenous than usual.

As we journeyed south, the weather took a drastic turn for the worse. The waves seemed as high as mountains and caused the ship to rock back and forth violently. The creak of the vessel as it leaned with each swell of the ocean sounded like a soft, soporific chorus. The water, though, churned and foamed around the boat like an angry sea monster trying to take it down and, in the background, there was the constant rumble of thundering rain.

The voyage was exciting but also very risky; it was like being inside a tumble dryer while riding a rollercoaster. It went on for days, but one morning, I awoke to an uncharacteristic and welcome stillness. There was no rocking from the ship, the wind had subsided, and an air of calm descended upon us. We had sailed beyond 60 degrees south and were now in a region of icebergs and pack ice.

Suddenly, the strikingly blue water was teeming with life, whales breaching and spraying water into the air while seals lounged on floating chunks of white around us. The sky, too, was alive with seabirds, their grey-white feathers vividly clear against the dark clouds.

In the distance, waddling Adelie penguins marched along in their tuxedo-like coats or glided effortlessly through the water, constantly moving and exploring their icy home. The cold air stung our lungs with every breath, sending shivers down our spines. Yet, there was a sharp exhilaration in the chill, one that invigorated our bodies and awakened our senses to the harsh reality of the frozen world around us.

The sun glinted off the ice, giving us a sense of being transported to another world - one that was far different from our everyday lives back home.

The crew huddled together, swapping stories and scrolling through a slideshow of photos from their previous expeditions to Antarctica. Each image was more breathtaking than the last – towering icebergs, an endless expanse of frozen landscape, the fierce waves during a storm, the vibrant hues of the sky and clouds, and the diverse array of wildlife captured in stunning shots of seals, penguins, and various bird species. We buzzed with amazement and anticipation as they shared their previous encounters in this isolated and frozen world. It felt like stepping into a hidden realm filled with tales of bravery, beauty, and peril, all captured in vivid photographs that seemed to transport us further into this enchanted land of ice. The landscape before us was a desolate beauty, stretching endlessly towards the horizon.

Shades of deep blue and crisp white mingled together on the calm waters, framed by towering glaciers. Majestic icebergs dotted the horizon like scattered jewels, some jagged and menacing, others smooth and gentle. We marvelled at their size and shape, all the while knowing that only a small portion of these massive structures were visible above the surface.

As we sailed, the immense ice floes moved in a mesmerizing ballet alongside our vessel, each boasting its own distinctive characteristics - some were small and circular, while others stretched for metres on end, their jagged edges reflecting the harsh conditions in which they had been formed.

Despite their differences, they all followed a graceful rhythm dictated by the ever-changing weather and ocean currents. These floating marvels were detached from any land or ice shelf, instead forming from the freezing seawater or breaking off from larger masses of ice. To the penguins and seals who called these icy islands home, they served as vital habitats and shelters from lurking predators.

As the ship approached our destination, it slowed, and the captain used the icebreaker to break apart the thick sheets of ice blocking our path. With expert precision, he led us closer and closer to our goal, until we were within five nautical miles.

The icebreaker needed to get us close enough to the station for the ice to be thick enough so that trucks could drive alongside and use a giant crane to offload the shipping containers, which were filled with food, equipment, materials, and scientific equipment necessary for life and research projects in isolation. The process took two days, and three helicopters were brought up on deck and used to transport half of the passengers to shore.

I couldn't believe my luck as I stepped onto one of the choppers, ready to take off from the deck. I was elated; it already felt like a once-in-a-lifetime opportunity. Little did I know that it was the first of several thrilling flights in the upcoming months.

I gazed through the windows, my heart pounding as I beheld the incredible grandeur of the icy sea sweeping out in front of me towards the horizon.

The sight was more breathtaking than I could ever have imagined - glacial floes rolled out before us like gossamer cobwebs, sparkling icebergs illuminated by the sun, distant glaciers towering imposingly in the background. The reverberating hum of the engines filled the air around us as we left behind the stalwart icebreaker and ventured onwards into uncharted territories.

Everything appeared still, but I could sense the anticipation mounting within me as we flew closer to our destination. Never had I witnessed such pristine magnificence before!

On station

The biting air stung my face as I disembarked from the helicopter. As it took off again, its blades stirred up the wind, leaving a trail of snowflakes behind. As I peered into the distance, I felt surrounded by an eerie stillness. Everything was blanketed in pristine white and sparkling like an icy winter fairy tale. The breathtaking landscape extended for miles before me. My pulse raced as I squinted into the featureless snow-covered horizon, but then I spied a red structure with its windows facing south. I knew it was the research station - my destination after almost fourteen days of travelling across the Southern Ocean.

A small group of expeditioners, bundled up in thick down parkas and fur- lined hats, marched toward me out of the building, the snowshoes on their feet swishing as they moved. We exchanged brief greetings before heading towards our destination and I felt the icy air fill my lungs as I trudged along.

When we arrived at the station, I stepped into an airlock to enter the building. It served as the "cold porch" where we took off our boots and outer layers and stored our weather gear such as beanies, gloves, and goggles. The cold porch also acted as insulation against any heat loss every time someone went in or out of the building.

There was a separate door allowing us to enter the interior space, where a bright lobby greeted us with its promise of warmth and comfort.

As I stepped into the station, I was welcomed by the muster board whose display provided critical information about who was on or off the station. The left side was adorned with tags bearing everyone's names written in black letters on white backgrounds, while the flipside had our names written in black letters on a red background.

They were all pinned to the corresponding room numbers to which they had been allocated, white background facing forwards, enabling anyone to easily find who they were looking for if needed.

The right side of the board was labelled "Off Station". Whenever someone left the station, their tag was taken from the left side and transferred to the right side (red side facing forwards) with all the necessary details about their departure time, itinerary, the communication devices they had taken with them, and their expected return time or date. In an emergency, this would make it easier for Search and Rescue team to deploy effectively and provide the necessary help. On returning to the station, the tag would then be pulled off from the right side and placed back under the corresponding room number, white side facing forwards.

The area was kept warm and cosy through a clever heating system that recycled the hot water generated from cooling the generator and sent it through an insulated network of pipes across the station.

Firstly, it circulated through the tank of hot water to ensure that the temperature remained consistent. A part of it was then diverted back outside, where it travelled at around 65-70°C through a bell-shaped copper device in a freshwater lake that usually stayed frozen year-round. When this hot water ran through the bell, it caused any snow and ice nearby to melt. This melted water was then pumped inside, filtered, and stored in tanks as our fresh-water supply. By that time, the hot water had cooled significantly.

The insulated pipeline continued to meander through the station, providing warmth to all buildings at no extra cost thanks to the clever use of water-to-air exchangers – one of the most efficient and eco-friendly methods of heating that I have ever seen.

Stepping away from the muster board, you found yourself in a large room composed of a dining area on the right side and a large commercial kitchen on the left.

The two sections were divided into a hot and cold self-serve buffet. Through the windows of the dining area, you could take in the dazzling view of the icy ocean, which would soon start to gradually melt away as summer approached. It was like watching a live performance on a giant movie screen, showcasing nature's ever-changing beauty 24/7. The scenery shifted all the time, depending on the movements of the clouds, icebergs, and the wind. Meanwhile, beneath the water, hidden currents gently moved huge chunks of ice in the distance. We were able to observe seals, penguins, and birds coming up close and personal, right to the heart of the station. Stormy days were just as thrilling; ominous dark clouds would roll in, and the howling wind from the plateau humbled us to our core. In those moments, we always trusted that the station had been constructed up to standard, so that we would be safe in even mother nature's strongest gusts. At times, the wind would blow at well over 160 km/h.

The dining area cupboards groaned with the weight of snacks like biscuits, chocolates, cookies, and instant noodles. Soon enough, on nights when we had indulged in a few too many homemade beers and played darts until the early hours of the morning, we would reach for this 'survival food' to get us through until morning. Even to this day, nothing can compare to the feeling of having indulged in a warm, gooey, cheesy sandwich straight off the grill, especially at night!

On the left side of the dining area, a glistening kitchen shone under the spotlights. It was equipped with more amenities than one might find even in a world-class restaurant - stainless steel appliances and countertops, a large double set stove-top gas burner, a combi oven, several individual walk-in cold rooms, freezers with moisture control for each different food category, a hot box/dough prover, and a commercial dishwasher. An array of carefully arranged spices and herbs lined open shelves next to sets upon sets of radiant pots and pans.

As I exited the dining hall, I walked up a set of stairs to the mezzanine bar area - a warm gathering place for conversation and laughter. There, I met Paul, who had been assigned two jobs: sparky by day and brewmaster by night.

He dedicated many after-hours, with the help of several eager fellow expeditioners, crafting our very own homebrew beers in what was known as "the brewery," an almost secret location in another building of the station. It was always exhilarating when we tasted the results of these experiments - some were scrumptious successes, while others were not-so-tasty fails.

Reflecting on it now, we could have undoubtedly qualified for a world record as the world's southernmost brewery!

Climbing up another short set of stairs, we arrived at a large open lounge area with multiple recliner chairs and floor-to- ceiling windows with the same majestic view as on the ground floor.

There was also a table tennis table, a pool table, and a dart board. Towards the other end sat a library, which was managed by our resident weather forecaster Leanne.

Right across from the library was our very own cinema, which was used for movies, presentations about research and science projects at the station, or just as a space for people to showcase past experiences or hobbies. I attended two talks in particular that captivated my attention.

The first was given by our resident doctor who had been one of the first responders to go and fight Ebola in Sierra Leone, while the second was from Rob, our resident plant operator, who had represented Australia in Precision Jumping - leaping from an aircraft at 1,000 metres and landing as close as possible to the centre of a circle measuring just twenty metres in diameter. Rob was passionate about base jumping and often went on trips to the French Alps or Chile for jumps; plus, he was an avid photographer and liked making short films about his exploits. His videos are truly amazing.

The main building was connected at the top to the accommodation one by an off-the-ground tunnel. Everyone had their own room and shared a bathroom and shower with the occupants of 3 or 4 neighbouring rooms.

Near the kitchen stood Steve's hydroponic gardening lab. This small setup would soon prove invaluable in our extended stay on ice, as it meant we could have fresh produce from his "gardens" when our supply of perishable goods ran low, and the next resupply wasn't due to reach us for months. I fondly remembered that in a few weeks, we would have some homegrown baby capsicum to enjoy in our salads, herbs to flavour our meals, and an array of cherry tomatoes and green beans. All 100% Grown in Antarctica!

Stretching out across the station were a few separate structures, each dedicated to a different task. There was a sewage treatment plant, laboratories for scientific research, an office for the weather forecaster, and a few other separate buildings such as a large workshop used by mechanics, plumbers, or electricians and a very large green building, which was our central storage facility.

The last structure in our little Antarctic community was the command building (comms building), where you could find our IT personnel, communications operators, operations coordinator, and station leader. If viewed from an elevated position near the station, it resembled a small hamlet of people living together in Antarctica's hostile conditions.

The first major task we encountered was unloading the icebreaker's precious cargo. We had all sorts of machinery and equipment to facilitate our projects and science programs, plus fuel for the electric generators. Most critically, though, there was a massive resupply of food to last us for the next twelve months.

Everyone worked together in a monumental effort, and the task was completed in less than three days.

The time then came to part ways with the outgoing team that had been on ice for six, twelve, or even eighteen months in some cases. It was an emotional farewell, and I felt genuinely emotional watching them board the icebreaker before we waved goodbye as it drifted away on the horizon.

Once the icebreaker had pulled away from our station, we were left alone in the remote wilderness of Antarctica.

A few days later, at about 1:30 am, the fire alarm sounded—and it wasn't a drill. In Hobart, before we departed, we had been instructed to prepare our emergency bags, which would contain basic survival items (I'm not talking about midnight cheese toasties here, but nuts, dried fruits, energy bars, dehydrated foods or chocolate, water, and extra clothing).

In the event of an alarm, we had to act fast: get our clothes on, grab our emergency bags, and rush to the primary assembly area. If it was inaccessible, there was a secondary alternative.

After arriving, there was a roll call that went on until everyone was checked off the list.

The blaring screech of the alarm had yanked me from a deep sleep, and I had fumbled for my emergency bag. The cold outside was biting as I hurriedly stumbled towards safety with my boot laces still undone and my jumper back to front. My heart was still racing as I finally got indoors with everyone else, taking several deep breaths to calm myself down. Sleep was the last thing on my mind at that moment.

Meanwhile, the firefighters had jumped into action. The expeditioners who would remain at the station over the winter had gone through rigorous firefighter training and were divided into two squads. Each team would take turns doing a week-long shift, which would mostly involve staying permanently vigilant and ready to jump into action in case anything went wrong.

The firefighting crew communicated with the station leader over their two-way radio and provided updates on the progress of the situation, eventually discovering it was a sensor malfunction that had triggered the alarm. After a while, we were eventually cleared to return to our rooms. But after being woken by the alarm, grabbing my bag, and walking through the freezing air to safety, I certainly wasn't planning on returning to sleep anytime soon.

It did, however, demonstrate the strength of our team when under pressure. We now knew we could tackle whatever challenge Antarctica put before us!

Although all fire alarms during my stint in Antarctica were false ones, I do remember hearing of a Brazilian base that almost completely burned down, with all personnel being rescued by the neighbouring Chilean station. It was a relentless reminder of our loneliness in this savage, merciless land.

The following morning, our field officers started field survival training for the new expeditioners. They took us out in packs of six and I was assigned to the first group. We were dressed in our windproof polar gear and Baffin boots with a set of ice crampons at hand, each of us carrying a backpack filled with a variety of supplies including dehydrated food, snacks, clothing, sleeping bags, a foam mattress, a pee bottle, a walking stick, sunglasses and sunscreen.

The last item might not seem logical, but the 24-hour daylight along with the reflection from both the sea and the ice meant that sunburn was a constant danger. I was about to embark on an adventure, and this was a whole new experience for me since I was much more accustomed to the kitchen than to the untamed nature all around us.

We studied how to use navigation tools like GPS systems and compasses as well as learning how to evaluate the safety of sea ice. We also practiced survival methods such as establishing temporary shelters, rescue techniques, and orienteering. We were blessed with quite clement weather as we stepped out onto the icy terrain, heading for Shirley Island and its Adelie Penguin colony. We had strict international rules regarding wildlife interaction to follow, which involved keeping a minimum five-metre distance from them at all times. Everyone was careful to follow these instructions and demonstrate our respect for nature.

After a quick lunch break on the island, we went back across the frozen sea ice toward the mainland to hone our GPS navigation skills. We then crafted a defensive wall made of snow and excavated some ice to make hot water for tea and dinner. I melted some pieces of ice in a pot on my MSR (a small, portable windproof burner). When the liquid was bubbling away, I added it to the dehydrated food inside its pouch, stirred the mix until it became unified, then closed the pouch again and let it steep for 15 minutes. Et Voila!

It had been roughly two-and-a-half decades since I'd last encountered dehydrated food, yet much to my delight, the modern-day versions seemed to have greatly improved in terms of taste and quality. Back then, rehydrating a meal was nearly out of the question; it was almost better to eat it dry, then wash it down with something like water, tea, or coffee. Bon appétit or, depending on the situation, bonne chance (good luck)!

After a day of scaling icy cliffs and slippery slopes, I was exhausted and found a spot near the ice wall we had built. I set up my bivvy bag - a lightweight cover for a sleeping bag (I joked that it was really just a glorified garbage bag.) I arranged my unrolled foam mat and polar-graded sleeping bag inside and used my backpack and hiking stick as support poles to give myself enough space to breathe.

The next morning, I felt surprisingly energised and ready for tea...but nothing ever comes quickly in Antarctica!

First, I had to bust up the ice like a mob boss breaking some unlucky guy's legs, then I threw the alu mug on the MSR burner and waited, with the patience of a saint, for the ice to transform into a boiling liquid. After what felt like hours, I finally got to enjoy my much-deserved beverage. As I kept an eye on the others, who were still blissfully asleep, I caught up with some of the other early risers.

Some had snored peacefully throughout the night, while others had tossed and turned like a ship in a stormy sea. Despite the surroundings, we were all in great spirits, knowing we would be at base soon for our well-deserved hot shower, and some nice warm food for our hungry bellies.

Back in relative civilization, time flew by, and the catering team, which comprised two other chefs and me, quickly fell into a rhythm.

We cooked for approximately ninety expeditioners daily, offering breakfast, lunch, and dinner options. Everything was prepared from scratch, and we baked fresh goods each morning.

Every day, crew members were able to indulge in a full continental breakfast followed by a few hot items for morning tea at 10 o'clock.

Lunch consisted of salads, charcuteries, and cheeses with leftovers from dinner plus a "soupe du jour" (soup of the day).

Dinner was a rotation of dishes like chicken curry, beef lasagna, and Mexican burritos; special requests were made for birthdays when feasible. Dietary needs were accounted for to ensure no one had an allergic reaction while in Antarctica.

I had to think outside the box when it came to substituting ingredients; swapping olive oil for butter or corn flour for all-purpose flour soon became second nature to me. What began as a challenge eventually became a daily learning experience that pushed my cooking skills in unexplored directions and resulted in me creating a range of dishes that everyone could enjoy. Little did I know that this experience would be so invaluable later on in my career.

As a professional chef, I had the opportunity to experiment with cuisines from all around the world, including pastries and baking. I was already very well-versed in this particular area due to my experience working on remote mining sites.

Having three chefs who specialised in different areas of cooking made it easier for us to leverage our collective knowledge. We rotated shifts so that we could maintain some variety while getting to know others within the station.

When I was on the early shift, I particularly enjoyed starting the day by baking bread every morning. I would turn off the exhaust hood and let the smell disperse throughout the building; even people who usually didn't have breakfast would suddenly appear, claiming they could smell it in their bedrooms.

There are two smells I adore: freshly baked bread and freshly ground coffee - they always remind me of my days spent in Paris when I was a young lad.

We had been discussing the importance of creativity in cooking one night over a game of darts and the conversation resulted in my deciding to make Mexican food the following week.

We ended up having enchiladas, burritos, and plenty of sangria – although there was no sour cream, so we had to use a mixture of cream and lemon juice to make our version.

Someone asked for guacamole, but we didn't have any avocados at hand. I remembered reading about a "fake" guacamole recipe with frozen peas in a magazine, so I decided to give it a go.

After cooking the peas, I added some of the homemade sour cream and lime juice to counteract the sweetness of the puree before adding chilies, garlic, coriander, diced Spanish onion, and tomato, and finishing it off with a hint of ground cumin to mask the pea flavour. I proudly presented the dish one night for dinner, and it had a few astute taste testers raising their eyebrows in confusion!

Nevertheless, everyone smiled and complimented me on the creation - it was not every day that someone served up mashed peas as guacamole.

Every month, expeditioners staying for the winter would receive a medical checkup. The occasion would always spark an amusing contest that we dubbed "Doc vs Chefs". While the doctor emphasised healthy living and eating, in the kitchen, we prepared all sorts of delicious cakes and cookies that were difficult to resist.

Most months, it was the Chefs who won. I can't remember anyone ever walking away from me skinnier - unless, of course, they had been running!

Since we had arrived, our work was not the only thing to take shape rapidly. Several gifted musicians had formed a band together, while I had joined another group devoted to planning events such as themed parties on weekends, Christmas and for New Year's celebrations (which came up quickly). We also arranged off-station trips, iceberg cruises, a mid-summer dinner, swimming in the icy Antarctic Ocean (yes, really!), a marathon, and Australia Day, with the end-of-season party looming not far behind. Outside of all this, if you had any other particular goal (as I did), you would need to find a bit of "you" time in order to accomplish it.

I had always been a passionate photographer, so I took any opportunity I had to spend more time with nature. The station was situated on an exceptional part of a rocky outcrop that offered plenty of safe places for hikes.

In this unfamiliar setting, life went by in the blink of an eye, and I realised it was important to manage my time judiciously between work and socializing to avoid becoming overwhelmed.

We had never been in a situation like this before, living and working together all day. Back home, everyone had their jobs, pastimes, and favourite spots; but at the station, we were all jammed together.

Although we were ecstatic about being there, tensions sometimes ran high. Lack of sleep also played a role in fatigue as well as emotions.

During summer in Antarctica, the sun continually circled above us without ever sinking below the horizon from mid-November until late January. It felt as if it was always lunchtime! I had even been caught playing darts at four in the morning when my shift was due to start within the hour.

On the flipside, the winter months would pose another great challenge due to the fact that, for around 6 weeks, the sun would barely rise, and it was all too easy to feel lethargic. All wildlife would migrate elsewhere in search of warmer climates, while the ocean would completely freeze over, only adding to the sensation of isolation. The station population would also decrease from summer numbers, down to only about 15-20 people.

One spot to take refuge during this trying time would be the hydroponic lab, which was kept at an ideal temperature and lit by UV lights, allowing plants such as herbs, cherry tomatoes, lettuce, and green beans to grow. During these times of extended darkness, appetites would change, and physical activity would decrease; it seemed best to mimic nature and enter a mini hibernation state, prioritising relaxation and self-care until the sun rose again and wildlife returned later in the year.

But for now, there was plenty of summertime left and the kitchen was the main hub of activity on station for two main reasons: For one, it was a warm haven from the cold outside, and secondly, there was always sustenance to be found there.

We upheld the traditions of early explorers, with only slight tweaks to adjust to modern life. In the book by P. Fitzsimons "Mawson; and the Ice Men of the Heroic Age," I read that expedition members took turns cooking and washing dishes, kept their living quarters neat and orderly, and continuously maintained the fire throughout the night. We refined the system a bit, assigning two people every day to "slushy duties."

This set-up worked wonders in integrating everyone with communal living and encouraging them to keep their surroundings clean. Plus, it gave individuals who might not have mingled otherwise an opportunity to connect; a doctor paired with a plumber, or a scientist with a plant operator made for plenty of diversity. The main tasks were usually washing up, restocking items for the dining room, tidying tables after meals, mopping floors, and cleaning public areas such as bathrooms.

As an incentive, those on slushy duty were allowed to choose or compile the day's playlist for the station radio. This would later become a humorous event, as other people on the station would be able to guess who was on duty just by the type of music playing. My good buddy Paul was known for his affinity for heavy metal, much to the chagrin of everyone else on the expedition.

But while the slushy team could decide which tunes to play, it was the chefs who had the final say on how loud it could be, so at least we had some say in the music - more so when it was ear- piercing. The second great motivator for the slushy team was that they got first bite of all the freshly baked goods, as well as the first pick of all the meals.

As a chef, it was difficult to make sure that everyone did their job correctly. Some teams were more productive than others - some people enjoyed staying indoors while others wanted to hurry up and finish the tasks.

At times, certain individuals found themselves having to perform jobs they wouldn't ever have considered in the real world. I remembered one amusing, if slightly embarrassing situation, where one of the crew came to me and said that the vacuum cleaner was broken. I was taken aback, as I had used it without any issues the day before.

We went up into the recreation area and I asked what was wrong with it; he replied that it wasn't picking anything up. When I inquired if he had emptied it recently, he looked at me strangely and said, "But it's a bagless vacuum cleaner – it says so on the side!"

Just above the spot where you would collect your plates and cutlery before dinner, a small piece of paper had been pinned to the wall. Its words read:

An Irishman walks into a bar in America and orders three whiskeys.
The confused barman looks around and says: "Waiting for someone?"
The Irishman shakes his head.
The barman then asks: "Well, would it be better if I put all three shots in one glass?"
The Irishman looks up and replies, "No! I have two other brothers back at home, so every time I go to a pub, I order a shot for each of them, too."

The following week, the Irishman comes into the bar and orders just two whiskeys.
The barman asks, "Did something happen to one of your brothers?"
"Oh no," says the Irishman, "I just decided to quit drinking!"

From my first expedition south, I learned the importance of maintaining high morale among everyone on the team.

To keep everyone's spirits up, I started a daily ritual of sharing jokes from a book I had brought along with me. Some were good and elicited hearty laughter, while others were so bad that they were amusingly bad.

Even though we were having one of the most incredible experiences ever, it was hard not to think about home and the people we had left behind from time to time. During our stint at the selection centre in Hobart, we were thoroughly briefed on the challenges and emotions that would come with leaving our families at home.

This was especially difficult for those of us with younger children; having a strong support system back home would be key in making the separation easier, which is why we strived so hard to keep everyone entertained and busy.

Sundays were the perfect day for a bit of respite, and they would start with a brunch offering to rival some of the best 5-star hotels.

On one occasion, I had arranged for a few small groups of explorers to embark on a scavenger hunt. The goal was to have a sort of progressive meal, so I had hidden three courses that each group would have to find by solving a series of riddles.

The activity took approximately an hour and a half and culminated in the return of the explorers to the dining hall, where I had already prepared some aromatic mulled wine that could be smelt from afar.

As chefs, we had an abundance of options to bring excitement into the mundane everyday life down there. On cloudy days, the delectable aroma of our cooking wafted through the air for miles. For instance, you could get a whiff of chocolate brownies from across the station and people would hurry back to the dining area as if it was their last meal.

We also had to use our creativity to make appealing dishes out of some of the less popular food supplies on hand.

I remember coming across some plant-based duck meat, and I knew the crew wouldn't find it too appealing if I told them what was in it. Instead, I called it "Vegetarian DUCK Stir Fry" with "Vegetarian" written in a small font and "DUCK" much larger. The meal was a tremendous success; in fact, only my friend Vas picked up on the wording and asked how a duck stir fry could be vegetarian. We laughed between us and kept it a secret!

Vas, who was affectionately known as "the Greasy Sparky", was an invaluable member of the expedition. A larger-than-life character with a loud laugh and a jolly disposition, his Greek heritage meant that he felt right at home in the kitchen. On one occasion, he and Paul, took it upon themselves to prepare breakfast so that I could sit down with everyone else and enjoy a meal that I wasn't responsible for making. What a treat it was!

Vas's favourite dish was slow-cooked lamb accompanied by zesty lemon potatoes and a generous helping of tzatziki.

On these occasions, he would be first in line for dinner. I remember one time; he filled up his plate and then walked off with the whole bowl of tzatziki! Whenever that "weasel" was around, there was never a dull moment!

Another time, a few people asked me if I could host some cooking classes to show them how to whip up breads, croissants, and English muffins, as well as how to perfectly poach eggs and make a Hollandaise sauce.

One guy explained that he wanted to surprise his wife with a home-cooked breakfast when he returned, since he never cooked at home. I'm still curious as to whether he ever followed through with his plan.

Saturday nights usually featured a more formal atmosphere, akin to a night out back home.

Everyone got dressed up, sometimes in smart outfits like shirts or suits (usually the more experienced returning expeditioners), but other times in costumes to fit the theme of the evening.

Dinner was served slightly later than on other nights, which gave us all an opportunity to catch up for a pre-dinner drink with people we didn't see during the week due to work and other commitments.

On certain occasions, the resident live band would play if there were talented musos in the group - I was fortunate enough to experience this on some of my trips down south. Once the band completed their performance, background music would resume over the speakers as people talked, played pool or darts, or watched a movie.

Saturday evenings had a jovial atmosphere, with laughter and conversations filling the room late into the night (or sometimes into Sunday morning). It made Sunday brunch even more logical, so people could enjoy sleeping in.

On the menu board next to the kitchen, we also always recognised someone's birthday. If we couldn't think of anything else, or if it was a spontaneous decision, we would make up a fake birthday for a person called Paul - which was usually quite amusing, considering how many people were named Paul on station.

I had become quite experienced in knowing what people liked, which meant that I could always put together a cake for everyone to enjoy. My three most popular were:

> *Lemon meringue tart:* A unique dessert consisting of a crunchy base filled with a refreshing lemon curd, topped with a sweet, silky Swiss meringue torched to perfection. *Yum!*

> *Traditional Black Forest cake*: A decadent multi-layer cake made of dark chocolate genoise "lightly" infused with Kirsch snaps, spread over with cherry jam, topped with whipped cream and scattered sour cherries, smothered around and on

the top with more fluffy whipped cream, and garnished with shavings of dark chocolate. *Yummier!*

Tiramisu: A base layer of Savoyard biscuits briefly infused in a mix of Kahlua and ristretto coffee, topped with a fluffy combination of egg yolks, sugar, mascarpone, and a touch of Marsala (or any dry white wine), finished with another layer of infused Savoyard biscuits and dusted with dark cacao powder. I like to make this dessert a least a day in advance to let the cacao powder infuse through the cake. *Yummiest!*

Friday afternoon Happy Hours were a delightful break from our usual routine.

Each department was given the chance to host, and everyone would always go above and beyond to make sure it was an enjoyable experience. The chef's team collaborated closely with the hosting team, providing delicious takeaway dinners that gave us all a much-needed change of scenery from the dining hall.

The lab scientists discussed their research projects while the Bureau of Weather Forecasting described their weather prediction models.

When it came time for the trades workshop's turn to host, the mechanics, carpenters, electricians, and plumbers created games to teach skills or provide entertainment. To top it off, they lit up the BBQ for everyone to enjoy, an event that was only matched by the aviation team's infamous Friday Happy Hours in the hangar, a homemade pizza delivery cart rolled up, much to everyone's excitement!

The aviation crew was made up of both airplane and helicopter pilots and mechanics (with several DC-3s, Twin Otters, and three helicopters). Kimba shared his knowledge about the machines' technical components whilst Paul walked us through the basics of piloting a helicopter.

But then everyone's attention shifted when the pizza delivery arrived. It was remarkable how something as simple as pizza could make everyone so happy.

The following Monday morning, I met with Paul the brewmaster and a few others over coffee, and he suggested that we meet at the station bar on Friday for our now-ritual Happy Hour, to celebrate the release of a new batch of homebrew.

We were discussing what to cook when Keiran started reminiscing about his experience in Munich at Oktoberfest, adding that it'd be great if I could make some pretzels. Growing up near Strasbourg in France, I knew pretzels well enough but had never attempted to bake them before; I would just walk down to the local bakery to indulge my cravings.

After searching the internet, I found a recipe and tried my first batch, but it wasn't a great success, so I searched for more recipes.

Of those I did find, the variations were very slight, and I couldn't understand why they were all failing. I tried researching bread-making in general when suddenly I recalled a conversation before leaving Hobart about how the extreme Antarctic climate affected the yeast in bread-making due to the low humidity in the air. Realising my mistake, I increased the amount of yeast and tried again.

After a few more batches, I was finally happy with the results and was looking forward to Friday night's Happy Hour to see if the others liked them.

A couple of days later, an unexpected visitor turned up, signalling its arrival with quite a roar. The sound of humming engines echoed out across the open wilderness, disrupting the tranquil peace that lay over us.

My eyes widened in shock as I saw a Chinook CH-47 transport helicopter, adorned with an Indian flag on its side, descend from the heavens and hover almost directly above me. Boasting two powerful engines capable of carrying 10,886 kilograms and 33-55 passengers, this impressive aircraft was not something to be trifled with.

I sprinted desperately away from the helipad, my feet barely touching the ground as an unstoppable force of snow and dust swirled violently around me, pushed onward by the deafening roar of the helicopter blades. The powerful winds created a vortex that threatened to rip me apart like a rag doll, sending me flying wildly off the helipad like a broken twig in a tornado.

The tradesmen working on the roof of a nearby building watched in awe and astonishment; it looked like something from an action movie!!

As soon as the engines shut off, the crew began to disembark. It was an official delegation from the Indian international research station.

We occasionally had visitors or travellers passing through on their way to their own station, including French, Italian, or Chinese citizens. It was always a pleasant surprise, and we welcomed this Indian delegation with the same open arms, giving them a tour of our station and its surroundings. The passengers spent the day with us, we had lunch together, and I prepared a box of treats for them to share with their colleagues back on the station. As a token of friendship, they then offered to take us out on a ride in the helicopter.

We left the station and flew south over the ocean and icebergs, veering east and passing by a glacier and fjord before returning safely to the docks. I was lucky enough to sit in the front cockpit, and I shared a laugh with them as I recounted my experience of their arrival earlier that day. The flight was short and extremely loud, but what an incredible experience!

After that interlude, Friday came about quickly. Everyone at the bar knew something good was coming because the appetizing smell of the fresh baking filled the air and spread throughout the entire dining hall. I showed up with trays of golden-brown pretzels and joined in on the tasting party.

The head brewer gave us a brief introduction to each beer that had been crafted onsite, how it was made, and which hops and malts were used in each one. As soon as everyone got their soft pretzel and beer, they took a bite and a sip.

You could hear a collective "Ahh!" as people tasted my creations for the first time. So magical was the combination that I coined a phrase: Pretzels and Beer, the Ultimate Best Friends!

I could not believe how successful my first public-facing attempt had turned out to be; it felt incredible to see people enjoy them so much.

We celebrated with more beer than usual and shared stories until late into the night - nothing beats good food accompanied by great company.

The night had been a fun and positive experience that left me buzzing with anticipation for the days to come. As I was chattering away excitedly with Keiran about everything we'd seen and tasted, I was caught off guard when one of my friends asked if I could make chocolate pretzels.

My initial scepticism quickly gave way to fascination as I considered the possibilities. Eager to take up the challenge, I enlisted a team of culinary adventurers and we set off on an exploration of flavour.

The kitchen was alive with laughter and enthusiasm as we crafted our concoctions from both sweet and savoury components, adding dips and drizzles to give each pretzel its unique personality. From classic milk chocolate to herb-infused gouda, no combination was too wild or wacky for us.

We followed a steady rhythm of work: communal duties, happy hours after work on Fridays, weekend activities, and time spent with those we were closest to.

The expedition comprised a motley crew that spanned both generations and professions. It was an intentionally eclectic mix, as the dynamic needed to have a balance of extroverts and introverts, youth and experience, men and women.

Over time, I grew nearer to certain individuals who shared my passion for food, wine, and good company. One such outstanding member was Sharon, our operations coordinator. Her boundless energy and drive fostered an environment of respect between the leadership team and the rest of us.

Even in the most demanding situations, Sharon never faltered – always keeping her cool under pressure. Tina was another. I met her at a selection centre in Hobart. We both attended the same week and went on to work together for two seasons. She held the position of communications coordinator, which involved liaising with those heading off-site as well as pilots during fly days. Tina had a warm, inviting smile that always put people at ease. Her remarkable talent meant she knew how to handle any situation without hesitation.

Then, there was Jen, the store officer who oversaw all our resources. She was always there for a helping hand. Without her, I would have been completely lost! Like Tina and Sharon, Jen was always in good form and had an encouraging demeanour that made us all feel better. These three were my nucleus, and as the weeks went by, we fell into a routine.

Before we knew it, Christmas had arrived! As chefs, we had been busy preparing a wide variety of treats for the upcoming festivities.

Just like back home, the station was transformed into a winter wonderland. The halls were adorned with sparkly lights, and festive tunes were played on the radio every day. The pace around the station seemed to slow as everyone took time to appreciate the season.

For some, this was their first time away from loved ones during the holidays. There was sometimes an air of sadness in quiet conversations and whispers overheard between colleagues.

But when the day of the party finally arrived, excitement filled the station once more. We all went for a plunge into the semi-frozen waters of Antarctica to start the festivities with a bang. Afterward, we had a few hearty snacks, including meat pies and vegetable pasties, in anticipation of our Christmas lunch later that day.

Before the main event, we reminded everyone to bring their Secret Santa gifts so that no one would miss out on any fun.

I remember bringing along a biography of Francis Birtles' "Australian Adventurer" as my gift; I thought it conveyed a sense of determination and bravery. When Santa finally showed up in his makeshift sled with his helpers, we couldn't contain our joy - I felt like a kid again! We each got a turn sitting on his lap to tell him why or how we deserved a present from him. After all the presents had been given out and unwrapped, we all headed back to our rooms to change into more formal attire.

The expeditioners all put on their fanciest clothes and gathered in the dining hall, ready to feast. Music filled the room as the decorators finished their work - streamers were draped from the ceiling, there were twinkling lights lit every corner, and a giant Christmas tree stood regally in the centre of the room, covered with decorations and glittery tinsel.

We took our seats at long tables that had been arranged by a group of helpful volunteers; each was laden with savoury dishes. The smell of freshly baked bread wafted over us as we grabbed our plates, which were piled high with hors d'oeuvres, cured meats and cheeses, vegetables and salads, honey-glazed ham, roasted turkey, and a delectable nut loaf. Every dietary requirement was catered for; from the most demanding fine cuisine "connoisseur" to our vegan diet-based colleague, we had it all covered. It truly was an extravagant banquet.

As we began to eat, it felt like time had stopped still. The atmosphere was electric; laughter and chatter filled every inch of space as we enjoyed every bite of the delicious food.

All around us, people were merry, and glasses clinked together regularly as toast after toast was made to celebrate love, joy, and friendship. It was truly a memorable day, and the first white Christmas for many of the group.

As I looked around at my fellow workers, it made me realize how much I had grown to care for them all since starting work here at the station. It felt so good to be celebrating this special holiday with such an amazing group of people, and even better knowing that once the Christmas festivities had passed, it was immediately time to think about the upcoming New Year's party.

During planning, we had decided on a Greek-themed event. Everyone worked hard to find decorations that fit the theme, and we put together some recipes to match. The station was transformed into a mini-Greek village, with national blue-and- white flags all over the walls. Music played from every speaker as people filled the dance floor, ready to move and groove.

Vas took charge in the kitchen and arranged for a large shipping container near the entrance, where he set up a rotisserie to cook his famous spit-roasted lamb while being sheltered from the weather.

The delicious smells of hot meat filled the air as everyone sat down at the tables, which were lined with platters of hummus, tzatziki, taramasalata, and more. A range of dishes like moussaka, lamb kleftiko, and pastitsio were served afterwards, followed by a classic Greek melomakarona cake.

When midnight arrived, we all went outside for one last party in the bright summer sun.

In Antarctica, during summertime, there was 24 hours of daylight, and the sun would be up high in the sky to welcome in the New Year. It was also the last show of the year from our resident band, and their performance was extraordinary as usual. We lifted our ouzo glasses to salute the start of a fresh year and sang our way past midnight. It was indeed an entrancing end to a memorable time.

January had been going smoothly until disaster struck!

One peaceful, sunny afternoon, everyone was occupied with their duties when the tranquil atmosphere was broken by a distinct alarm; not a fire alarm, but the "search and rescue" alarm.

In accordance with the procedure, and understanding that this wasn't a drill, we all congregated in the dining hall, anticipation and fear brewing among us.

Our station leader then divulged the news: one of the aviation crew had had an accident, and the search and rescue team was on its way. The impending hours tightened every nerve in the station like hot wires, paralysing us with an overwhelming sense of fear. The atmosphere grew so heavy that silence blanketed the once bustling hub; where laughter and smiles normally filled the air, nobody uttered a word as they waited anxiously for whatever was to come.

The next few hours felt like an eternity until a call came through on the radio informing us that the missing crew member had been found and retrieved but was severely injured, and that everyone from the search and rescue team and the aviation team was now on their way back into station.

As we waited, the atmosphere was tense and sombre. When they finally arrived, we could see that the injured crew member was in critical condition and needed immediate medical attention.

The station's small medical team sprang into action, rushing the injured crew member to the clinic. It was a race against time, as they had been outside for a long time.

For the next few hours, the station was on edge as we waited for updates on their crew member's condition. Despite the circumstances, though, we all pulled together to support each other and maintain the running of the station. We took turns to cover each other's duties and made sure that morale remained high.

But then, the news that we all dreaded, and that no one wanted to hear, arrived.

The station doctor had declared the injured crew member deceased. It was an announcement that sent shockwaves through us all.

The sudden realization of the finality of death was overwhelming and heart-wrenching; it seemed almost impossible that something so terrible could have happened right there, in such a tight-knit family.

Yet, despite our pain and grief, we had to keep going. We held a wake for the lost crew member the next day and spent the evening reflecting on what had happened while honouring their life. A veil of silence stretched across us as we quietly reflected on the agony the family must have been going through back home.

Though it was a heavy day filled with emotion, we felt grateful to be able to find comfort in each other's company as we paid tribute to this fallen expeditioner. It had clearly shaken us all to the core. We had never experienced such tragedy on station before, and it served as a chilling reminder of what could happen to us in the harsh and unforgiving environment.

Indeed, it changed our outlook on the dangers of life in an isolated and unfamiliar place; no matter how careful we were, something could still go wrong. It was a constant reminder that we needed to stay vigilant and not take anything for granted. We were reminded that even under the worst circumstances, it is important to keep going and weather any storm together.

As time passed, we slowly moved on from the unfortunate incident but always remembered what happened in respectful silence; it was an event that would stay with us forever.

From then on, one thing became clear: no matter how tough things got at the station, we would always remain resilient and continue onward, no matter what else came our way.

Out and about

The sun kept shining day and night, providing us with an abundance of opportunities to go outside and explore this barren yet splendid continent.

I took advantage of these endless days and went out as much as I could—it would have been a shame not to make the most of our time there. I was in awe of nature's sublime power and humbled by the feeling of being so small in the presence of something so vast. I felt a deep sense of gratitude for the opportunity to explore this uncharted territory.

One of my preferred places was the Vestfold Hills, an area of 411 square kilometres on the north side of Sorsdal Glacier, on the Ingrid Christensen Coast of Princess Elizabeth Land. The hills there are subdivided by three west-trending peninsulas, enclosed by narrow fjords. Most of the peaks range between 30 and 90 metres in height, with the highest summit reaching nearly 160 metres, and the landscape is dotted with a great variety of water inlets with over 300 lakes and ponds, comprising what is possibly the largest concentration of meromictic (stratified) lakes in the world. The geology tells the story of a complex and unique environment where gneiss formed from ancient sediments and magma 2.5 billion years ago, then metamorphosed under high pressure and temperature, eventually forming dolerite dykes 1.2 billion years ago.

It is an Antarctic oasis, largely free of ice or snow, with many lakes and ponds containing distinct chemical and biological features. When the sea ice melted in summer, an array of wildlife would emerge. From squawking penguins to various types of seals (Weddell, southern elephant, leopard), and birds like the South polar skua or snow petrels— it was a never-ending source of entertainment right before our eyes. My favourite creature of them all was the Adelie penguin. These tuxedo-like birds, with their black and white plumage, sleek bodies, and defined white circles around their eyes were captivating. During my first visit, I couldn't resist taking over a thousand photos of them.

Not too far away from the station were a few huts that you could hike to and stay for a night or two. They were big enough to comfortably fit 4-6 people, making it an ideal opportunity to spend some quality time with your closest friends.

On the opposite side of the station muster board, there was a board with the names of all the huts listed. If you wanted to join an existing group, you could place your name under the hut that had available space; if you had enough people, you could reserve an entire hut for your own party. Weekends were naturally busier than weekdays, since most people had Sundays off.

I, however, tended to work on weekends, so it was easier for me to book a spot during the week. I asked my friend Paul if he wanted to join me and enjoy some time away from his obligations mid-week. For safety reasons, there had to be at least two people travelling out of the station, one of which needed to have sufficient experience to be a trip leader. Before we could go to the hut, we had to map out our route, make sure we had functional communication devices and GPS systems, arrange all of our food and drink needs, and pack our bags with everything we needed for the journey, including a survival kit in case we got caught in bad weather.

Paul and I browsed through the store, picking out food for our upcoming trip. We grabbed some dehydrated meals that would be light and easy to carry in our backpacks. At one point, Paul pointed to a tin of steak and kidney pie that looked like flying saucers and asked what they were. Curious, I read the back of the tin before we decided to take a risk and try them out. As a chef, I didn't have particularly high expectations, but since I enjoyed a good steak and kidney pie, it was worth a shot. We were serious about the expedition and wanted to make sure we were well-prepared.

We set off early on a clear Wednesday morning, our backpacks loaded with food, extra layers of clothing, and all the necessary equipment.

The hike took roughly six hours across the rocky terrain. The landscape around me captivated my attention with its endless shapes, colours, and lines. Our journey took us past pristine meromictic lakes that shimmered in the sunlight, their still waters reflecting the majestic hills that surrounded them.

Just like with the penguins, I couldn't help but take countless photographs of this incredible scenery of rocky valleys, crystal clear lakes, and the bright sun against the navy sky, illuminating the majestic white icebergs in the ocean, which were mirrored by distant glaciers against dark hills. It was completely mesmerising. A hike through the Vestfold Hills in Antarctica is truly an unforgettable adventure for anyone who loves nature and exploration.

When we finally made it to the hut, we placed our heavy backpacks down and it felt like a breath of fresh air. Then, we started getting ourselves settled in and warming the place up before planning the next two days.

Our plans were slightly altered, though, as we noticed a sudden change in the weather. On contacting the station, Tina confirmed that there was indeed bad weather heading our way for the next 12 hours. After unpacking we decided to try out the steak and kidney pies that we brought with us. The instructions said to take the lid off and heat the pie in its tin for 20 minutes in the oven, so we followed those directions. To our surprise (mostly mine), they were delicious! The pastry was flaky, the filling was tasty, and the combination of steak and kidney was a match made in heaven.

We sat in the warmth of the hut, enjoying our meals and chatting about all the incredible experiences we had had so far on the trip, and then we got out a pack of cards and embarked on a games night - something I hadn't had experienced since my childhood growing up in France. Here, though, in Antarctica, I rediscovered that simpler life - one where card and board games were central to basic enjoyment. As the night wore on, we crawled into our sleeping bags and drifted off to sleep, the sound of the wind lulling us into a restful slumber.

The next morning, as we set off on our hike towards the highest peak, the sun was shining brightly, and the air was crisp and clean. I took a deep breath and felt rejuvenated by the pureness of the air in such a remote part of the world. The hike itself was challenging but rewarding, with steep inclines and rocky terrain that required focus and careful footing. But as we reached the top, all of our efforts immediately proved worth it as we were greeted by breathtaking views of the fjord below us, and mountains in every direction. We took some time to rest and take in the beauty around us before heading back to the hut for lunch.

As we walked, we came across a group of adorable Adélie penguins waddling across the ice. They seemed to be just as curious about us as we were about them, stopping now and then to look at us before continuing on their way. I couldn't help but smile at their playful antics.

After a quick lunch break back at camp, we decided to further discover the nearby surroundings. We spent the afternoon exploring the area, admiring the incredible rock formations, taking in the stunning views, and observing more penguins as they went about their day. As we walked along the shore, we stumbled upon a seal basking in the sun, completely unfazed by our presence. It was a surreal experience to be so close to a wild animal in its natural habitat. As we made our way back to camp for dinner, I couldn't help but feel grateful for the incredible opportunity to explore such a wild and untouched place.

Both days were fairly similar, filled with hikes, lots of snacks and wine, plenty of photos, playing cards, and having great fun. Little did I know that my ever-growing collection of pictures would come in handy later in life, and even give me the chance to make a little money on the side. The final evening was bittersweet as we prepared to pack up our bags and head back to the station in the morning.

The following morning, as we were preparing to hike back, we overheard a conversation over the radio between a helicopter pilot and the station. As we listened in, we couldn't believe our luck. The pilot had just completed a food drop-off to keep three scientists, who were living in a field camp on a nearby island, stocked up. We saw this as an opportunity and quickly interjected, asking if there was any possibility of hitching a ride back to the station.

To our amazement, the pilot agreed and said he would pick us up from our hut in a couple of hours after finishing his tasks for the day. We were thrilled at the thought of saving ourselves from an exhausting six-hour trek with heavy bags. After packing up our belongings and saying goodbye to our cosy little hut, we eagerly awaited the arrival of the helicopter. Finally, we heard its distinct sound approaching in the distance and soon enough, it landed right outside our hut. We hastily loaded our bags and climbed aboard, excited for a different kind of adventure.

As we took off and flew above the hilly landscape studded with countless lakes, fjords, and glaciers, I couldn't believe my eyes. We could see for miles in every direction, with endless stretches of white ice and snow broken only by jagged rocky hills. I felt like I was in a dream as we flew over valleys and glaciers, being treated to an incredible bird's eye perspective of the entire Vestfold Hills area. Before long, we were descending towards Davis Station, where we were greeted by smiling faces and warm hugs from our friends who had stayed behind.

One of the most thrilling activities on station was cruising around icebergs on zodiacs.

We had the chance to do this once or twice a year, usually in January when it was the warmest, least windy time of year. One day, after having indulged in our usual Sunday brunch, the perfect opportunity presented itself for us to start on a new expedition. It was a captivating experience that necessitated thorough preparation: all the appropriate safety gear had to be present, and everyone had to wear Mustang suits for warmth and dryness. These thick, bulky items of clothing were made from neoprene and nylon, with tight rubber cuffs at the wrists and ankles. They kept us insulated while we beheld the extraordinary scenery.

Before embarking, every passenger was asked to get their survival bag ready and go through a short safety briefing. As our boat glided across the shimmering waters, we were hypnotised by the beautiful icebergs in their many shapes and sizes, all bearing intricate natural designs. Some seemed almost transparent, offering us the chance to try and peer beneath the above-water peaks, while others were cloaked in snow, adding even more beauty against the bright blue sky. The largest ones were truly colossal.

The Zodiac moved steadily through the icy depths of Antarctic waters, past yet more icebergs with colonies of penguins perching on top. On land, they appeared somewhat clumsy, but when they entered the sea, they became proficient swimmers, requiring all that agility to evade potential predators like leopard seals or sea lions. Some snow petrels and Antarctic skua soared through the wind with grace.

As our zodiac manoeuvred past a series of floes, someone suddenly noticed something unusual. A small family of Weddell seals had congregated upon a single piece of the glacial expanse. Most were dozing off in the warmth of the sun, while two young pups curiously peered at us from afar, their fur showing tinges of light and dark brown, along with a few hints of white. Their large eyes blinked in wonder as they observed us closely through their thick eyelashes.

They didn't seem scared or timid; on the contrary, they were clearly filled with curiosity and eagerness to explore their visitors. We silently entertained ourselves as we watched the seals interact with each other as if it was nothing more than an everyday routine for them –

communicating through grunts, sliding around on their bellies, and occasionally splashing water around with their flippers.

The young pup nearest us decided to make its way closer towards the zodiac, giving everyone a better view of its features before blending back into its family again at a safe distance. It was one of those moments when time seemed to stand still, and everyone onboard was transfixed, waiting in silent anticipation of another glimpse, before we eventually had to get moving towards even more exciting explorations ahead. That Sunday iceberg cruise remains with me to this day.

As we turned back towards the station, I felt immense gratitude for the experience.

The beauty of the wildlife and icebergs, as well as being so close to penguins in their natural habitat, was truly special.

That day, I knew deep inside my heart, that I would never want to see those beautiful creatures anywhere else than out there in the wilderness, where they lived, played, and belonged.

Message in a bottle

Back in the station, next to the board with the names of all the huts was a large, very detailed topographic map of the nearby area. I had been examining it for days, trying to find a place with a perfect view for my landscape photography.

I went out on many expeditions and encountered all kinds of wildlife along the way. It wasn't always what I was looking for, but each trip gave me plenty of chances to snap pictures and document my journey.

At the time, my nephew Louka was only 6 years old and living back in my hometown in France. He was so proud to tell his friends that not only did he have an uncle living in Australia, but he was also embarking on adventures in Antarctica!

I chuckled at the thought of his excitement. It was true - I was living a life many could only dream of, and as I continued my search for the perfect spot to capture the beauty of the landscape, I couldn't help but feel a sense of excitement. In my search for the Holy Grail of photography, it felt like I was on a treasure hunt. The loot was the perfect moment for a picture, and the many obstacles to the goal were like those we faced as kids playing games around the neighbourhood.

It all brought back memories of my childhood when my friends Joel, Olivier, and I would embark on adventures in our small town.

We would climb trees, explore the woods, and build forts. It was all so simple back then! But now, as I braved the harsh terrain of Antarctica, I realised that even as an adult, I was still on that same adventure, just on a much grander scale.

After a while perusing the map, my attention was drawn to an itinerary I thought could be interesting. It wasn't too far from the station, so I decided to make the hike and explore on my own. I would take a path between Lakes Dingle and Stinear until I reach Lake Weddell, then pass Camp Lake and walk to Powell Point. According to the map, the elevated location would provide great views.

To the southeast was Brooke's Hut, which was nestled along a fjord leading out into the Antarctic Ocean. It was in line with BR-05, which was a good reference point during GPS navigation.

It all seemed to be an ideal spot for a stunning panoramic landscape photograph. With my camera in my backpack and armed with all the required safety equipment, some food, a lot of water, comms, a GPS, and a sense of determination in my heart, I set off on my journey towards Powell Point.

The hike wasn't easy, as the terrain was rough and unpredictable. The snow had accumulated in some areas, and I had to be careful not to fall or lose my balance. As I trudged forward, I couldn't help but feel a sense of awe at the sheer beauty of the landscape. The blue sky stretched out endlessly above me, and the silence was all-encompassing.

I was so lost in the natural beauty that I didn't realize I had reached Lake Weddell until I was standing right by it. The lake was so glassy, it looked like a peaceful blue mirror. I saw two confused penguins standing there and I couldn't help but think they were trying to figure out who the odd one out was - me or them. It was like nothing I had ever seen before, and I knew I had to capture it on camera.

I remember that day very well as all the colours seemed even more vivid than usual. I spent hours taking photos of the lake and the surrounding landscape, making sure to get every angle and every detail. Eventually, I started making my way towards Powell Point, eager to see the panoramic view from the top.

When I finally got there, I was breathless, the view was just spectacular. The fjord that led out into the Antarctic Ocean stretched out endlessly, and Brooke's Hut was nestled beautifully along the shoreline. The blues of the sky and ocean were highlighted by the countless icebergs of various shapes and sizes, creating a stark contrast to the rocky terrain I was standing on.

After trekking for hours to get here, I was running out of time. The wind began to pick up and I knew I had to hurry if I was going to get the shot I'd been waiting for. I got going, making sure to take multiples of each angle and when I finished, I stored my camera in my backpack, took a swig of water, and readied myself to head back to station. With a growing sense of urgency, knowing how unpredictable the weather could be, I hefted the bag onto my back.

Right before I left, something peculiar caught my attention. Despite being in the rocky outcrop since morning, I noticed a specific cairn (a pile of smaller stones), about half a metre in size, that looked like they had been stacked by human hands. To my mind, someone had definitely carried them to that spot and carefully placed each one on top of the other, as if working on an art project. It certainly didn't look like anything natural.

With careful and deliberate movements, I began to shift the heavy stones, one by one. As they rolled and crumbled under my touch, a glimmer of curiosity sparked within me. And then, I saw it - a hidden container nestled deep within the earth, its white surface reflecting the light of the sun, beckoning for me to uncover its secrets.

My heart raced with excitement as I reached out and gently brushed away the dirt and debris that had concealed it for so long. What treasures or mysteries lay inside? The possibilities seemed endless, and I could feel a sense of adventure stirring in my soul.

As I opened it, a small piece of paper fluttered out and landed at my feet. The paper was faded, but the words still felt tangible, as if they were now part of the landscape. The letter read:

"Passed this way on my way back to Davis after walking out via Lake Dingle, Weddell Camp Lake.
I made this little monument and dedicated

it to my 2 children, Samantha and Darren, and to West Ham Utd, the
greatest football team in the world. I, Roy, wintered here in 1983-84.
I am an electrician and helped build the store building at Davis with the
rest of the crew Darrel - Keven - Colin - Bear - Max - Phil - John - and
Brum.
Only two weeks to go before our boat comes for us, thank F: @K!
Hope you had a great year; Davis station is the best. I live in Melbourne."

As I was reading it, my heart was pumping with excitement. It was such a strange feeling to read Roy's heartfelt words, he must have loved his children dearly to have made this dedication to them in such a remote place.

I remembered my own childhood once again and realised that finding the piece of paper from 30 years ago had left me feeling like Indiana Jones all over again. This paper was my real-life Holy Grail. There was no monetary value in it, but it didn't matter the slightest. The fact that I could connect with Roy, who had been at that exact spot over three decades ago, made me feel as if he were there with me at that moment, sharing his incredible journey with me.

Every intricate detail of his letter made him come alive in my mind; from the mention of the itinerary and his children to the names of his colleagues and even the football team he supported - West Ham Utd!

I attempted to put the document back in its container, but the cover snapped when I tried to fasten it. I assumed it had to be due to the decades spent exposed to the harsh conditions of Antarctica. I did my best to fix it and placed it back at the bottom of the pit, carefully replacing the stones on top of the container before continuing on my way back to station.

I tried to imagine what Roy's experience must have been like all those years ago, but I felt a pang of guilt knowing that the letter wouldn't remain safe in its broken container for another winter down here. I decided I had to go back and replace it with a new one. I impatiently awaited my next day off so I could revisit the place where

Roy's monument had stood. I had taken the time to document its GPS coordinates, which would make my return trip a much faster one.

The day I had been waiting for had finally arrived, and I had procured a suitable container in preparation. It was strong and came with a solid lid, which was hinged on top. I also thought it would be a nice gesture to add a note to Roy's letter.

Unfortunately, on that day, all plans to leave the station were cancelled because a blizzard was headed our way, making it hard to even stand outside the main building, let alone venture off on a lone expedition. The thought of not being able to go back within two weeks had me feeling worried.

Though the weather was far from ideal, and visibility was greatly reduced, I decided to take a chance and swap out the containers before it was too late. It was my last shot!

As I was on my way to the spot, I thought about how fragile our lives are, yet equally, how important they are for so many others along our path. The little letter had reminded me of how powerful memories can be, and it had touched me deeply. Although we would never get to meet each other, I was sure Roy would have been satisfied knowing that someone had found and cherished his dedication to his family 30 years later.

I moved quickly, not wanting to be caught out by the weather conditions, and I made it to my destination in record time. To my relief, the note was still intact, and I switched it out as quickly and carefully as possible. As I made my way back to the station, a thought began to grow in my mind, and with nothing else to do, it quickly became an obsession.

Could I get in touch with Roy's children, Darren and Samantha, about my discovery?

Back at the station, I went down the hallway and found a picture from the year that Roy had been on the wintering team. It was thrilling to put a face to the name.

On station, communication opportunities were excellent. We had great internet access and social media at our disposal, so it didn't take me too long to find both Darren and Samantha's information.

As I exchanged messages with Darren, the anticipation and excitement grew inside me. I couldn't wait to share my discovery with him - something that had once belonged to his father, Roy.

His response was immediate: "Dad will be stoked!" My curiosity got the better of me, so I asked: "How is your dad?" The reply warmed my heart even more: "Dad is doing well; we're planning for his 80th birthday celebration in a few months!"

A surge of emotions rushed through me, and I smiled to myself. It was heartwarming to know that Roy was still alive and well. Lost in thought, I wondered what I could do for him on this special milestone. As I scrolled through gift ideas, one thought kept resurfacing - I wanted to give him something meaningful and personal. With determination in my heart, I sent a message to Darren asking if it would be alright for me to reach out again in a few months when I was back in Australia. His reply came quickly, filled with nothing but warmth and understanding.

Our conversation concluded positively, both of us looking forward to the upcoming meeting in Melbourne.

It was now late February, and we were all eagerly awaiting the arrival of the Aurora Australis at Davis station to take us back home. Excitement filled the air as our attentions turned to seeing our families and loved ones again, after a long time away. Before we could get too carried away with our plans, news reached us that the Aurora had already reached Mawson station to resupply the team there and collect expedition members who had finished their time in Antarctica.

The original plan was for the ship to make a quick stop at Davis to pick us up after leaving Mawson before heading back to Hobart. However, things took a turn when we received word of a major setback - a relentless blizzard had struck the station, its icy winds whipping across the rugged landscape. The icebreaker had lost its hold and was sent hurtling towards Horseshoe Harbour, where it slammed into treacherous rocks. Although the ship sustained no major damage, safety concerns loomed, and the crew could not now risk taking on any expeditioners.

As summer drew to a close and options for departure dwindled, desperate measures had to be taken; namely, reaching out to other Antarctic programs for rescue. It didn't take long to find kindness in the shape of a Hercules LC130 aircraft from the US Antarctic program, which was willing to brave the harsh terrain and fly to Davis station to pick us up and return us to their McMurdo Station 2,600 km away in the Ross Sea.

From there, another plane would be chartered to transport us back to Australia before winter set in. The stakes were high, and time was running out - would we make it back home or be stranded in this frozen wasteland?

In Antarctica, everybody needs a plan B!

After much rushing around and plans changing almost every half hour, the Hercules finally arrived and within about five hours, we had landed at McMurdo, the bustling US hub of Antarctica. Again, though, we were met with the unfortunate news of bad weather looming on the horizon for the next few days. It was another disappointment for us all; after spending countless months away from home, all we wanted was to return to familiarity and warmth.

However, as seasoned adventurers by now, we understood that Mother Nature was in control and there was little we could do but make the most of our stranded situation. It turned out that being stuck at McMurdo wasn't so bad after all.

The small town, which mostly consisted of research facilities, essential infrastructure, and even a chapel, offered us an opportunity to explore its unique surroundings and get up close and personal with

Scott's base, which was named after the legendary polar explorer Robert Falcon Scott.

Despite the harsh weather conditions outside, we managed to capture some breathtaking photographs of the impressive landscape around us, including Mount Erebus, the world's southernmost active volcano. In between two bouts of bad weather, a few of us even made it up to Observation Hill, which is home to a nine-foot wooden cross that bears the names of those who perished on Scott's final expedition, as well as the last line from Alfred Tennyson's poem, "Ulysses":

"To strive, to seek, to find, and not to yield."

The cross was erected on the summit of Observation Hill, facing out towards the Ross Ice Shelf where Scott's party had tragically met their fate in 1912.

Our fearless leader Jamie, hailing from New Zealand and no stranger to extreme climates, reached out to Scott's base and arranged for us to tour their station and even share a meal with them on one of the evenings. It was a heartwarming gesture that brought a sense of camaraderie between two groups of people in such isolated conditions. My partner-in-crime and fellow chef, Jarrod, jumped at the chance to showcase our cooking skills for dinner at Scott's station. The resident chef graciously accepted our offer, although he hardly needed any help as we were to discover that he ran his kitchen with military precision. Nevertheless, we were happy to lend a hand and show support for our fellow explorers in this unforgiving land.

After four days of relentless blizzard conditions, the weather finally cleared and the once-tumultuous sky transformed into a vibrant shade of crisp blue, a welcome change from the icy turmoil that had plagued us for what felt like forever.

We eagerly awaited the arrival of the chartered Airbus A319 from Christchurch (New Zealand), arranged by the AAD. Huddled together in our cold, well-worn gear, we could feel the excitement building as we waited for the aircraft.

The flight from McMurdo to Hobart was a once-in-a-lifetime opportunity. As we boarded the A319, we couldn't help but feel a sense of awe and anticipation for the journey ahead. We were told that the route would take us about 4,500 km due north along the Transantarctic Mountain ranges, which would offer spectacular views of this remote and largely untouched part of the world.

As we took off, we braced ourselves for what would surely be an unforgettable experience. We were not to be disappointed!

The first leg of our journey took us over the Ross Ice Shelf, an enormous floating ice sheet almost as large as France. It was quite a sight to behold, with its vast expanse of white interrupted only by sporadic cracks and crevasses.

We then flew over the Transantarctic Mountains, which rose imposingly from the ice below. These mountains are some of the most isolated and inhospitable in the world, which made it feel all the more incredible that we were flying over them. As we reached our cruising altitude, we were treated to breathtaking views of the deepest inner reaches of Antarctica. We saw incredible blue ice fields stretching out next to us, only broken up by isolated nunatak and frozen glaciers.

The landscape below us was constantly changing as we flew further north, and after almost five hours, we finally crossed into Australian airspace and began our descent towards Hobart. As we moved through the thick clouds, excitement buzzed through our group. The thought of returning to civilization after months in such extreme conditions was almost surreal.

But even as our adventure came to an end, none of us could deny how fortunate we were to have witnessed Antarctica from such a unique perspective.

The business setup

When I returned to Australia, everything felt different. Life on the frozen continent was full of excitement and unexpected moments, not to mention the great company and fascinating wildlife I encountered every day.

My homecoming was far from satisfying. The scorching heat and high humidity on the Gold Coast took me by surprise. Even though it was late March and already autumn in the Southern Hemisphere, the temperature remained in the low 30s while the humidity was over 90%. It was impossible to even stand up for any length of time without feeling completely drained. The cold climate had become so familiar to me that I almost felt dizzy. I was dehydrated and lacked the energy to even take a shower, let alone search for a job.

But then, I remembered the one thing I missed most during my time in Antarctica: the sensation of the ocean breeze on my skin. I envisioned the refreshing feeling of a salty wave washing over me, the coolness of the water beneath, and the smell of the sea. A surge of enthusiasm washed over me, and I decided to take my two furry companions, Paquita (a female Border Collie) and Poppy (a male Toy Foxy / Jack Russell cross), for a walk to the beach and a dip in the ocean. With an overwhelming sense of joy, I stepped out of my house and headed towards the sea with two excited dogs beside me.

After all, it's common knowledge that the Gold Coast boasts some of the most stunning beaches in the world. As soon as we arrived at our destination, Poppy and Paquita dashed into the waves while I followed closely behind.

The cool water enveloped us, providing a refreshing escape from the heat. It was such a liberating feeling, just the three of us playing in the ocean without a care in the world. As we ventured further out, dolphins and seagulls joined in on our fun little adventure. We stayed in the sea until the sun began to set, basking in the moment until we all felt completely rejuvenated.

On our journey back home, my attention was caught by a newly opened microbrewery. Memories of Antarctica flooded back to me - our homemade beers and pretzels after a long day of work. I decided to go home and take care of the dog's evening routine before returning to the brewery for a well-deserved drink.

The beer I tried surprised me with its smoothness and flavour; it was clear that they had put great effort into their craft. It felt like a small piece of that special time had been brought back into my life once again.

Hours passed as I chatted with the manager of the brewery; the bar had been quiet on this typical mid-week evening, which suited me perfectly. We talked about my time in Antarctica and shared stories about our favourite home-brewed beers. My stomach was growling, but there wasn't much on the menu that appealed to me. So, I told the manager about the Pretzels I used to make on station and how they would have paired perfectly with the beer selection there. He chuckled and suggested that I should bring some over, as they would surely be a hit with his patrons. As laughter filled the quiet surroundings, signalling an end to our exchange, I decided it was time to head home and start searching for work the next day.

The weeks ticked away as I looked for employment, but I had ample money from my time abroad, so I wasn't too worried.

I had also been preparing the perfect present for Roy's upcoming birthday. I had found an old piece of driftwood which I sanded down to serve as a sturdy base for my gift. The centrepiece was a panoramic landscape photo taken at the location where Roy had left his letter, under the small monument dedicated to his children. The wood perfectly contrasted with the bright vivid colours of the blue sky and ocean, as well as the white of the frozen fjord and icebergs. The rocks blended in beautifully with the background. In the centre, right below the picture, I fixed a metal plate with the GPS coordinates engraved upon it. Lastly, I covered the whole thing in epoxy resin to protect it and make it easier to transport when the time came to take it from the Gold Coast to Melbourne, where Roy lived.

Time flew by in a maze of job applications, but I began to realize that my attempts at job hunting on the Gold Coast were in vain, as it was off-season and most businesses in the area were catering to tourists.

I decided to venture north where corporate companies were more prominent and more jobs were therefore available.

My journey took me up to Brisbane, a city roughly 80 kilometres away. The first thing I noticed upon arriving was the sheer difference between this metropolitan hub and the tourist-oriented Gold Coast.

The city seemed to be overflowing with career opportunities and bustling with people. The streets were filled with high-rise buildings that housed some of Australia's largest corporations. Everywhere I looked there were people dressed in smart business attire: suits, ties, skirts; ready to take on their daily responsibilities.

I finally managed to secure a job interview for the following Wednesday morning with a reputable entertainment establishment located in the heart of Brisbane's Central Business District (CBD). It was perfect timing as I had just messaged Darren to let him know that I was coming to Melbourne that weekend to deliver his dad's birthday gift. We had agreed on this plan while I was still in Antarctica. Weekends spent in Melbourne were always enjoyable for me. There was so much to do - I could attend a sports game, check out a comedy show, visit bars and clubs or, most importantly, indulge in some of the amazing restaurants.

As a chef, I loved discovering new places that offered the latest culinary trends. The quality of food and service in Melbourne was truly impressive, both at the high end of fine dining and the smaller cafes that were dotted around the city.

Searching for rooftop bars was one of my preferred hobbies – something I had picked up when I was on holiday in Europe. I was pleasantly surprised to discover that Melbourne's own offering was pretty amazing. The views, both during the sunset hours and at night were unmatched - something that was hard to find elsewhere! The trip taught me that sometimes it's worth exploring your own backyard, as you can always find wonderful places without having to go too far away.

But there wasn't an enormous amount of time to explore as, after months of anticipation, I was finally ready to meet the person with whom I had shared a secret treasure chest buried in the wilds of the Vestfold Hills. I was both excited and scared - what if he was a grumpy old man? Or what if we didn't like each other? But those worries faded away as soon as Darren and Roy showed up. It was disappointing that Samantha hadn't been able to make it that day, as she had prior commitments.

Nevertheless, the project that had begun in Antarctica was now coming to an end.

I knew who Roy was immediately because of the picture I had seen of him at the station. His politeness and well-mannered demeanour instantly put me at ease; it was almost like talking to an old friend who I hadn't seen in years. He had a very neat appearance and spoke with confidence.

We found a spot to sit down and talk for a couple of hours. I took out my laptop and showed him some photos of what the station looked like now compared to when he was there thirty years prior. He was eager to learn more about all the new structures that had been added, and I enjoyed explaining them to him. I gave him three photo albums filled with pictures of the beautiful landscape we had both hiked through: one for him, and the other two for Darren and Samantha. I had also managed to find a small manuscript that contained photos of the expeditioners who were with him thirty years ago, along with a few sentences about their lives.

He became emotional upon seeing it, remarking that it was nice to see considering his memory was fading. Then, I gave him the original container that had held the letter many years ago, and he was amazed to see that it was still in my possession.

Finally, I presented him with the "pièce de resistance": the picture I had taken from the location where I found the container with his letter. It looked beautiful!

We spent hours talking and I didn't even notice that it was almost lunchtime. We were all hungry and thirsty, so I suggested we go to a nearby restaurant where we could continue our conversation while eating. I was feeling great that day as the whole experience had exceeded my expectations.

Things seemed to have fallen into place perfectly, and meeting Roy and Darren had been a wonderful experience. Roy turned out to be an incredibly interesting person, especially given the circumstances. My goal for this meetup had been achieved, and we had a fantastic time eating, drinking, and enjoying each other's company before it was time to say goodbye and I waved Roy off as he headed home to the suburbs. It was an intense but beautiful moment between us, and as I watched him walk away, I knew I would always hold onto the memory.

After such an eventful day, I decided not to head straight back to my rented apartment for the weekend. Instead, I made my way to Goldilocks Bar in the heart of the city, eager to watch the sunset while relaxing with a drink. As I was nursing my beer, two distinct thoughts crossed my mind: One: The upcoming job interview. Two: Would this be the last time I ever came across something as exciting as a hidden note from Antarctica, or would fate lead me to discover more compelling stories?

I was now back home; it was bright and early on a Wednesday morning in May as I settled into my seat on the train and began my journey to Brisbane for the interview.

Despite reflecting on the amazing weekend in Melbourne and reminiscing about the delicious food and wine I had shared with Roy and Darren, my thoughts soon shifted to the task ahead of me.

I was fully aware that there were limited chef positions available where I lived, so this opportunity would require more travel; yet I still hoped that I could impress enough to get the job.

The interview went on for well over an hour and the panel conducting it were enthralled with my tales of Antarctica, and the images I had on my phone. It was clear that they were deeply affected by my experiences and accomplishments. We talked about the challenges of living in Antarctica, the long days and nights, working in extreme weather conditions, and the sudden changes to our daily lives as we adjusted to life at the research station. My storytelling gave me a newfound appreciation and admiration for life-changing expeditions such as mine.

The experience had not only pushed me out of my comfort zone but allowed me to see a world I would have otherwise never known. I also shared how meaningful it was to find the container and the letter, and I told them about my recent trip to Melbourne to gift Roy with the keepsakes of his time in Antarctica for his birthday. At last, after conducting their final round of questioning, they thanked me for my time and wished me luck with my future endeavours - whatever they may be! With that, I said goodbye and left their office feeling very satisfied with the conversation we'd had. I thought I had a good chance at getting the job, but to be honest, I wasn't sure if I wanted it.

The venue was the most popular hangout in town, but it would mean I'd have to travel for over an hour each way and work long hours. But that had been my only job opportunity so far, and I knew I needed to start making money soon.

Having skipped breakfast and with lunch still some time away, I decided to take a walk in the downtown area, hoping to find something to snack on. As I walked up Queen Street Mall, the amazing scent of popcorn wafted into my nostrils. Although I wasn't usually a popcorn addict, the odour made me think I could eat a whole bucket of it right at that moment! That wonderful smell of popcorn was like some kind of heavenly aphrodisiac. And then I saw it; the source of that sweet scent was none other than the weekly farmer's market at Reddacliff Place.

The market was bustling with activity, and I strolled through, taking in all the sights and sounds. Vendors were selling all sorts of fresh produce, meats, cheeses, and baked goods. The air was filled with the aroma of herbs and spices, and my mouth started watering as I made my way through the crowds. One vendor caught my attention in particular; he was selling artisanal popcorn in a variety of flavours, so I sampled a few different varieties and ended up buying a bag of the spicy jalapeno to snack on as I continued my walk.

As I progressed through the bustling market, I found myself fully immersed in its dynamic energy and the diverse mix of people from different cultures, ages, and backgrounds. It was a melting pot of activity, with something for everyone to enjoy. Suddenly, a thought struck me with such intensity that I felt almost dizzy: "What about pretzels?" With almost panicked anticipation, I backtracked through the entire market, scanning each stall in search of my prey like an eagle on the hunt.

Nobody was selling pretzels at the market! As I stood there in the midst of one of Australia's major cities on a busy Wednesday afternoon, memories flooded back of the positive feedback I had received from my fellow expeditioners during our time in Antarctica just a few months ago.

That's when it hit me - why not start a small business selling freshly baked pretzels at the market?

Thanks to our experiments in Antarctica, I knew that offering a variety of choices - both sweet and savoury - would be key to success.

And so, just six hours after arriving in Brisbane for a job interview, I found myself sitting on the train heading back to the Gold Coast without a job, but with an exciting business idea instead.

On the train, I began jotting down sketches and notes, creating a list of tasks and things to consider. I needed a business plan, a list of equipment, licensing considerations, costs and, most importantly, a business name! It needed to be unique, timeless, modern, and easy to remember. After brainstorming over 20 potential names, I finally settled on *The Pretzel Nook*.

The day had been long and eventful, and the heat and humidity only added to my exhaustion. As I sat down at home with a cold beer in hand, I looked over the scribbles from my train ride back to the Gold Coast. I made a list of urgent tasks before eventually dozing off on the sofa, finally succumbing to the heat and my fatigue.

The next morning marked the beginning of a lengthy process to turn an idea into a successful business. Years ago, during my night shifts in the mines across Australia, I had completed an online course for a Diploma in Project Management without any specific reason. Little did I know that one day, it would come in handy for this project. With my background in project management, I was able to apply efficient methods to save time, resources and costs, while also identifying constraints and legal requirements, managing finances, and getting a few stakeholders involved.

After a few days, I had compiled a list of necessary equipment for my business venture: a 3x3 marquee, a mobile freezer, a convection oven, a small fridge, trestle tables, display baskets, cooking trays, and a few other miscellaneous items. With the equipment identified, I then needed to find the right vehicle to transport it all.

After carefully considering the size, shape, and weight of each item, I determined that a long-wheelbase van would be the most suitable option. I narrowed down my choices and sought advice from my friend Paul, who was an expert mechanic currently stationed in Antarctica.

Despite the distance, we were able to communicate thanks to the station's strong internet connection.

After discussing my options with him, I decided on the Renault Trafic LWB van. It had been my first choice anyway, and I had already seen an ad for one on a car sales website. When I mentioned the asking price to Paul, he encouraged me to act quickly before someone else snatched it up.

The following morning, I visited the dealership and became the proud owner of what I affectionately called *"The Pretzel Van."*

The next step was purchasing the remaining equipment. My previous experience as an Executive Chef at Sea World Resort and Water Park on the Gold Coast had given me knowledge about commercial catering suppliers in the area.

However, one challenge I had identified early on was dealing with the weight of some of the equipment - particularly the benchtop freezer. After buying the product, I had to travel 30 km to the transport company's warehouse for pickup, as they did not offer delivery to residential addresses. While it was disappointing and inconvenient to receive this news, going to the warehouse myself solved several of my problems.

The following day, I arrived at the warehouse with no idea how to load or unload the benchtop freezer from my van. I could have asked friends for help, but that was not a feasible long-term solution. After signing all the necessary paperwork, a friendly receptionist directed me to the back loading dock where my item was waiting. The store officer didn't ask any questions about how I wanted the freezer loaded. He just disappeared, returning a few minutes later on a forklift carrying the heavy commercial freezer, which weighed 120kg empty.

My mind raced as I tried to figure out how I would handle such a weight, but while I was contemplating, the store officer simply drove the forklift right up to the van and gently placed it inside. I was amazed at how effortlessly he had handled the task. Then, he looked at me from a distance and shouted, *"Have a great day mate!"* before driving off through the loading door, which closed behind him.

I stood there, feeling numb with a mix of excitement and apprehension.

The first part of the problem had been solved so simply. But now, I faced the challenge of unloading it alone.

As I struggled to secure the freezer in the back of the van, a 4x4 truck pulled up in front of the factory. The driver was a landscaper with a ride-on lawn mower on his trailer.

Watching him for a moment gave me a sudden realization: what I needed was a ramp to load and unload equipment. On my way home, I stopped at Supercheap Auto and bought a pair of bike ramps. Problem solved! It's funny how sometimes, by pure coincidence, we stumble upon solutions to seemingly insurmountable problems.

All the pieces had fallen into place: I had transportation, secured the necessary licenses, registered as a small business owner, and my friend "P" was working on branding and website design. Plus, I had identified my target market. Things were starting to come together nicely.

So, on Sunday morning, I baked some samples of my pretzels at home and casually made my way to the Arts and Crafts on the Coast market.

My goal was to meet the market organizer and convince him to give me a spot at the market since no one else offered a similar product.

As I arrived, I easily located the management tent and saw a strong man with dark hair, tanned skin, and a beard standing under the marquee. My heart sank as I saw him surveying the area with a tight and serious expression. I cautiously approached, my mind racing with apprehension and determination. There was no mistaking it: he was the key to my success, and I had to convince him at all costs.

The market was extremely popular and almost impossible to get into; it was held every Sunday in prime locations by the beach. I decided to approach the challenge with the same go-getter attitude that had landed me a job in Antarctica.

With newfound confidence, I walked up to the big fella, who was now sitting in his camping chair under his marquee.

"Good morning, my name is Seb. How are you today?" I greeted him.

"G'day mate, I'm Damon. How can I help you?" he replied, without paying me much attention.

"You look hungry, so I brought you breakfast," I said, handing him a box filled with warm pretzels that had just come out of the oven less than 30 minutes before. *"Breakfast? Really?"* the man replied, finally looking up at me. I took this as my chance to pitch my product and convince him to let me be a stallholder at his market.

I told him about the origin story in Antarctica, and how it had become such a success among the people on station. But it quickly became apparent that Damon wasn't interested in my sales pitch; I could well have recited the Ave Maria prayer in French, and he wouldn't have noticed as he was so completely focused on the breakfast that I had brought him.

As soon as I realised this, I knew I had him hooked. *"Are you available for next Sunday's market in Burleigh Heads?"* he asked.

"Of course, I am," I replied confidently, despite not being entirely sure if I could actually make it. But this was too good an opportunity to pass up.

"Great, see you bright and early next Sunday. Set-up is at 5:30 am and the market runs from 7:30 am until 2:30 pm....Oh, and it's our busiest one," he added.

"I'll be there - thank you for the opportunity," I said before turning and walking away, not wanting to interrupt his breakfast any longer.

The pretzels had worked their magic, but I also had a lot of preparation to do before next week's market. The week flew by at an unrelenting pace – to be expected with a looming deadline - but everything fell into place in time for the event and on Saturday evening, at around 9:00 pm, I finally felt ready. The excitement and nerves kept me from getting much sleep that night. I lay there, constantly running through checklists in my head to make sure I hadn't forgotten anything.

By 3:30 am on Sunday, I couldn't stand it any longer and got up to make myself a cup of coffee. Of course, I did one last check just to be sure. As I drove out of my garage, memories of my grandmother's sister flooded once again my mind, with her signature phrase "One day, on a nice day." And now here I was, one day, on a nice day, heading towards a turning point in my life - my first attendance at the local market in Burleigh Heads, where I would be selling my freshly baked pretzels.

Setting up my stall took longer than expected, but as the sun began to rise, everything was in place. A batch of pretzels came out of the oven right on cue, coinciding with the appearance of the early-morning marketgoers.

The delicious smell wafted through the air, quickly drawing people to my stall. It was a moment of relief - today was make or break for my small business venture, and there was no room for mistakes. Success was crucial. Fortunately, it was a resounding success, as evidenced by the fact that I ran out of stock just after lunch. Some customers were disappointed, but when they asked if I would return the next weekend, I enthusiastically replied with my signature catchphrase:

"Yes, of course!" Clearly that answer was a bit premature, as my future appearances at the market were ultimately dependent on Damon. I hadn't seen him since earlier that morning, but a few minutes later, I spotted his silhouette in the distance approaching my stall.

"So, Pretzel Guy, how did it go?" he asked in his deep voice.

"It went well," I replied. *"I sold out of all my pretzels and received great feedback from regular marketgoers".*

Damon then informed me that I had been highly recommended by several patrons for a permanent position at the market. The news filled me with joy, and I couldn't help but smile.

"I'd love a permanent spot on your market every Sunday!" I exclaimed. Damon said he would be in touch during the week before walking away. It felt like mission accomplished – not only did I have a successful first market day, but I had also secured a regular gig and could now relax at home with a few celebratory beers.

The next morning, I woke up feeling groggy and hungover. It was weird because I hadn't drunk much the day before - just a few beers - but I still felt awful. I stumbled my way to the kitchen and chugged down a big glass of water.

My body felt dehydrated and in desperate need of fluid. I grabbed some Berocca tablets, hoping they woul give me a boost of vitamins and minerals, and let them dissolve in another glass of water. As I sat on the bar stool, leaning against the counter, I watched as the tablet slowly disappeared in the water.

It suddenly hit me why I felt so horrible - I hadn't had anything to drink during yesterday's market, despite the hot, sunny, humid weather. Being a stallholder at a market was no easy task. You had to wake up early, drive to the location, unload all your equipment, set up your stall, cook and sell simultaneously, interact with customers or try to gain new ones, then pack everything up at the end of the day, drive home, and unload everything again. There was no time to eat, drink, or even take a toilet break. It was not a job for the faint-hearted.

After an hour or so of rehydrating, I began to feel much better, so I decided to tally up the earnings from the market. Although it had been a good day, I realised I needed to attend more markets per week for my business to be sustainable.

Based on my re-budgeted forecast, I determined that attending three per week would cover expenses such as stall rental fees, council taxes, costs of goods and packaging, and travel costs for my van (including fuel, parking fees, registration and insurance, and wear and tear). However, after researching nearby markets on the Gold Coast, I discovered that they were all held on Saturdays and Sundays. Since

I already had a spot secured for Sunday, I needed to find a spot for Saturdays.

But even then, how would it be possible for me to attend three markets when they were all held over two days on weekends on the Gold Coast?

After a few minutes of racking my brains, I remembered the Wednesday market in Brisbane City, where the idea for my pretzel business had first come to me. Without wasting any more time, I searched online for "farmers markets - Wednesday - Brisbane" and found the Jan Powers Farmers' Market website, which was the organizer of that event at the time. Scrolling through their website, I found an online application form to apply to be a stallholder and filled it out without hesitation. This was the only midweek market operating in Southeast Queensland, which also meant there would be fierce competition to secure a spot.

The next morning, my phone rang while I was busy tending various tasks. I didn't recognise the number and assumed it was a telemarketing call, so I hesitated to answer. But on the last ring, I had a change of heart and picked up.

"Good morning, may I speak with Seb? This is Jason from..."

I didn't catch the rest, but it sounded like a sales pitch, so I politely responded:

"Good morning, Jason. This is Seb speaking. Sorry, where are you calling from?"

"Hi Seb, I'm calling from Jan Powers Farmers' Market in Brisbane. I'm the market manager," he replied. My heart raced with excitement. Could this be my lucky break?

Trying to sound nonchalant, I replied, *"Hey Jason. It's nice to hear from you. How's your day been?"*

"It's been good, thanks mate. I noticed that you applied for a stallholder position at our city market on Wednesday; is that right?" he asked. I hesitated before responding confidently, *"Yes, that's correct".*

" Well, I took a look at your website and your product is certainly unique. Unfortunately, there aren't any available spots at the moment. We've got a long waiting list and not much turnover - some of our current stallholders have been with us for 2, 3, 5, or even 10 years."

My hopes were shattered in less than 30 seconds. I couldn't even muster a reply. After a long pause that made me fear I had lost the connection, his voice finally came back to life.

"I do have an opportunity for you though, but it's at quite short notice," he said, interrupting my thoughts. *"I'm hosting an event at King Georges' Square next week and someone just dropped out...would you be interested in taking their spot?"*

Without hesitation, I replied with my usual attitude, *"Yes, of course, count me in."*

"That's great news, Seb! I was worried it might be too last minute, but your product description caught my attention, and I'm excited to have you on board. I'll email you all the necessary paperwork immediately." Then, he added, *"However, since we're so close to the event date, I need your payment for the stall by close of business today. Is that okay with you?".*

"Absolutely, no problem," I replied. *"I'll fill out the paperwork and make the payment within the next couple of hours,"* I assured him before ending the call. I immediately went online to find out more about the event location and was thrilled to discover that it was being held at King George's Square, one of Brisbane's top public squares, located right in front of City Hall and only 300 metres from the main Wednesday market location at Reddacliff Place.

Luck seemed to be on my side once again...at least for now!

Within an hour, I had received all the necessary paperwork from Jason, and I promptly filled it out and returned it.

As I read through the event description, I realised that it wasn't just a one- day event; it would be running from Tuesday at 5:00 am until Friday at 5:00 pm. This was a huge step for me, going straight from my first-ever market right into a four-day, back-to-back event. But what concerned me even more was the fee for the event - it was ten times more than the cost of my Sunday market.

Still, the potential to make an awful lot more money made it seem worth it, and I could still fulfill my commitment to Damon's Sunday market.

I wasn't sure if I could afford it, though. In fact, when I looked at my bank account, I only just had enough money to safely pay for the Sunday market stall rent. If I went ahead with Jason, I would have had nothing left - no safety net, no backup plan. It wasn't the first time I had faced such a predicament, and it certainly wouldn't be the last. But despite my concerns, I knew I had verbally agreed that would attend, and as old-fashioned as it may sound, I never backed down from a commitment. This time wouldn't be any different. After filling out all the necessary paperwork and transferring the money to book my spot, I only had one thing left to do: prepare for a busy week ahead.

I increased pretzel production, while still having to make them on my kitchen counter at my house in Miami.

As I worked frantically, I quickly noticed that after that week, I would need to find a more suitable space for production.

My business model was simple - I made the dough, shaped the pretzels, and froze them before packaging them in containers in my mobile freezer.

On market days, I would load up the van with the freezer and other equipment and drive to the market site. After setting everything up, I would cook the pretzels and display them for customers to grab and go. This process took less than 10 minutes and was incredibly efficient compared with other vendors. It meant that customers could watch me bake their pretzels right before their eyes, and the process would fill the air with delicious aromas.

It was a unique and captivating show that set me apart from other market vendors.

Before I knew it, Sunday had arrived and it was time for my second market with Art & Craft on the Coast, this time in the nearby suburb of Broadbeach.

The unique aspect of Damon's Market was its rotating location every Sunday. Despite the location change, though, we were always on a beachfront site, which attracted both regular marketgoers and tourists alike. As the Gold Coast is one of the top tourist destinations in Australia, we were never at a loss for customers.

On Sunday morning, I woke up bright and early, ready to head to Broadbeach, where Damon was busy marking out stall locations on the floor. Upon arriving, he immediately approached my van with news that there had been a dropout, and he had a spot for me next to the popular coffee trailer.

I was still new to the market scene, but I had quickly learned that every stallholder wanted to be placed near the coffee vendor as it was the busiest area. Damon noted that my stall had a high turnover rate and customers didn't have to wait long for service. In fact, many used the opportunity to browse my products while waiting for their coffee. This was one of my greatest strengths - I could handle all aspects of running my stall alone, from cooking and presenting to interacting with customers and making sales. I even joked that the longest part of the process was waiting for the eftpos transactions to go through!

That Sunday was even busier than the previous one, which was exactly what I needed to add a little extra cash to my bank account. I made sure to stay hydrated this time, knowing that Monday would be a busy day as well, and that Tuesday through Friday would be extremely demanding at the event at King Georges Square.

On Monday afternoon, I received an email from Jason with various instructions and times. My allotted time to set up was between 5:00 and 5:30, which meant that I needed about an hour and twenty minutes to drive to Brisbane from home, and another thirty to forty minutes to get ready before leaving. I set my alarm for 3:00 am, realising as I did that this was something else I had overlooked when setting up my business: market stallholders need to be a mix of night owls and early birds!

As I arrived on Tuesday at around 5.15 am, I introduced myself to Jason as *"Seb from the Pretzel Nook."*

He greeted me warmly, thanking me for joining on such short notice.

"Not a problem, Jason – I'm used to it!" My answer was only half true; while I wasn't used to last-minute changes as a business owner, I was certainly familiar with the concept from decades working in hospitality. I had learned that you just have to jump into the water if you want to swim - and that's exactly what I was doing. I quickly unloaded the van, parked it offsite, and went back to set up my stall.

My routine was now well-honed, and I found that I made the process of setting up and packing down more efficient with each market.

By 7:00 AM, the city was bustling with people going to work or school and I had already made several sales. Other stallholders seemed surprised by how many customers were stopping at my stall. From the beginning of this business venture, I wanted to offer a grab-and-go experience for customers rather than making them wait for their food. This not only encouraged impulse purchases but also kept a dynamic energy buzzing around the stall.

As a market visitor myself, I hated waiting in line for food, which was why I wanted to focus on all-day snacking rather than just mealtimes, like many other food stalls did. At other stalls, customers would have to read a menu and imagine what the food would look like. Then, they'd place an order, pay, receive a number, and wait (hopefully patiently) for their order to be called up. Even then, there was always the risk of your order getting lost or mixed up. I refused to accept this hassle. I figured that if I had to stand waiting in a market for my food, I might as well go to a nearby restaurant where I could sit comfortably at a table and enjoy a glass of wine while my order was being prepared.

Market food, in my opinion, should be quick, fresh, one-of-a-kind, reasonably priced, and easy to eat on the go. It appeared that the marketgoers agreed with me, too, as everyone was opting for pretzels. The morning rush was pretty consistent until 9:00 am, when the flow of customers abruptly stopped for almost an hour.

It dawned on me that the city workers were now at their desks, students were in class, and tourists and day visitors were probably still yet to surface. This gave me a chance to chat with Jason, who was impressed by my products and the efficiency at the stall.

He informed me that today and tomorrow would be the slowest days of the week, while Thursday and Friday would be extremely busy. He also suggested ramping up social media advertising for the event. As expected, the rest of the day and Wednesday brought average sales. I couldn't help but feel disappointed, as my earnings from the first two days barely covered the cost of renting the stall. I knew that we had to make a profit during the last two days of the event, and that meant we would need a substantial increase in customers.

One of the main perks of the event was that Jason had arranged for overnight security to patrol the premises, saving us the hassle and physical labour of packing up each day. It meant I could get a decent night's sleep before Thursday, when I wanted to arrive at the stall by 4:00 am.

As I set up and began cooking pretzels, I noticed that there were no other vendors around yet - only the nighttime security team. As soon as my first batch of pretzels was ready, a few people approached my marquee. It was a mix of site security guards, employees finishing their night shifts at nearby hotels, and even some patrons who had just stumbled out of the casino after a long night of gambling.

Someone in the crowd asked if I was open yet. *"Absolutely,"* I replied with confidence.

And just like that, before any other vendors had even arrived, I was off to a great start for what would turn out to be one of my best days of pretzel sales at any market so far. Jason was right - it was going to be a busy two days!

My countertop was handmade with all glass panels that perfectly displayed all the different flavours I had for the day: jalapeno, smoked paprika and cheddar, cheese and herb, classic sea salt, cinnamon sugar-coated, chocolate chip, and blueberry frangipane. I also set up a tasting area at the front of my marquee and word spread quickly about the unique selection available and the delicious dips I offered at my pretzel stall. Customers were amazed and the blind taste tests got a particular amount of attention, with groups queuing up to guess the flavour. It was incredibly fulfilling to see people's faces light up with joy as they tasted my pretzels; it felt like a major accomplishment.

Thursday was a huge success, so I decided to start even earlier on Friday, at 3:30 am. Just like the day before, there were still night owls roaming the city centre and business was booming straight away.

By 1 pm, I had sold out of all my pretzels. As it happened, that turned out to be perfect timing because, after that, the market started to slow down, with people wanting to get to work early on Friday morning so they could leave the office earlier in the afternoon and avoid rush hour traffic.

After packing up my stall, I searched for Jason to thank him for the opportunity. He was talking to a large, tanned man who looked like a mafia boss from afar.

Jason called out to me, *"Hey Seb, let me introduce you to Joe. He's the market manager at the Powerhouse farmer's market in Newfarm."*

I greeted the man and he said, *"Hi Seb, I was just speaking to Jason about your stall. Are you free on Saturday?"*

"Tomorrow?" I asked.

"Sorry, not tomorrow," Joe clarified. *"I meant next week - there's an available spot right next to the coffee trailer at our market and I think your quick turnover would do very well there."*

I replied, *" You can count on me! I have been looking for a Saturday morning gig so this will work perfectly. Thank you so much, Joe."*

I shook both men's hands, went to my van to start the return journey to the Gold Coast. Despite a busy and tiring week, I was feeling energised after my conversation with Joe. The opportunity to start a new market the following Saturday had got me excited; things seemed to be falling into place without me having to push too hard. It felt like it was meant to be.

I spent all of the next day organising my equipment and restocking ingredients in preparation for my regular Sunday Art & Craft on the Coast market. However, I also knew it was time to find a better production space for my pretzels, as working from home was no longer feasible.

By chance, I came across an advertisement for a sub-lease in the same suburb where I lived, less than half a kilometre away.

Without hesitation, I called the number and spoke with Kate, the owner of the space. She agreed to meet with me within the next two hours, and after seeing the location and meeting her, I knew it was a perfect fit. I quickly sealed the deal with her on the spot. Suddenly, by Monday, I would have my own production space. It was a thrilling turn of events that seemed almost too good to be true!

Just like every Sunday, the market was off to a busy start for me. Amidst the hustle and bustle of dealing with clients, I caught sight of Jen and Vas from the corner of my eye. They had just returned from Antarctica a couple of weeks before and had decided to spend their weekend on the Gold Coast, surprising me with a visit to the market. It was so great to see them again. The last time we had seen each other was when I left at the end of summer, while they had stayed behind to winter on the station. Clearly, something had sparked between them during that time as they were now a couple. It came as no surprise to me; I could sense it even when I was still in Antarctica. Unfortunately, I couldn't spend much time with them since I was busy with clients, so we said our goodbyes with a quick kiss. But as quick as it had been, their surprise visit made my day.

As the week came to an end, I was tired but satisfied with how productive and fruitful it had been. The next few days were spent settling into my new production facility, making fresh pretzels, and preparing for the upcoming weekend markets at Powerhouse and Art & Craft on the Coast.

Saturday started early once again, as we had been told that the time, we could gain access for setting up (called "bump-in" in market-speak) for the Powerhouse market was 4 am.

After a quick shower to wake up fully, I headed straight to Brisbane's Newfarm area where the market was being held. It was 2.20 am, so the road was virtually empty, and I had no trouble making my way to the Powerhouse.

When I arrived on site, I could both see and hear Joe in the distance. He may have looked intimidating at first glance to a bystander, but he was a kind-hearted person who would do anything to help someone in need. He noticed me and motioned for me to follow him.

He led me to a spot next to the coffee trailer and said, *"Try it out today and give me a call later this week. If you like the location, it could be your permanent spot."* I thanked him and promised to call in a few days.

As I started unloading and setting up, I saw that the girls running the coffee trailer were already well ahead of schedule and no doubt would be starting to serve soon.

After introducing myself briefly, I worked quickly and tried to catch up on them. Instead of my usual routine of preparing everything before starting cooking, I had a gut feeling that I needed to change things up that day.

My risk paid off almost immediately as I got the first batch of pretzels finished just in time for the first coffee orders and, sure enough, customers waiting for their drinks also decided to purchase some pretzels as a snack.

People were thrilled to see a variety of both sweet and savoury options in one spot near the coffee trailer, and I knew this would be a prime location for my business. The day flew by, with me constantly running around trying to keep up with demand. When I finally glanced at the time, it was already 11:30 am and I had almost sold out of everything.

In the distance, I could see Jason approaching me. We quickly caught up as I finished selling my last pretzels.

It turned out that one of the stallholders at the city market on Wednesdays had had to drop out due to health issues, and Jason wanted to know if I would be interested in taking their spot.

It felt like a dream come true, and I eagerly accepted the offer. Jason said he would call me on Monday to discuss details.

This stroke of luck followed an already successful three weeks in which I had managed to secure three markets - Wednesdays, Saturdays, and Sundays - which was exactly what my business needed to thrive. The Sunday market turned out to be exceptionally busy with school holidays and visiting tourists, but I felt confident in my ability to set up, cook, sell, and pack up smoothly thanks to my growing base of loyal customers.

I knew with the new markets starting next week, my life would settle into a comfortable routine. I had secured regular markets and a steady source of income.

Each week would flow into the next seamlessly, and I couldn't have been happier. Even though it had not been an easy job, it didn't matter as I hardly considered it as work; to me, it was the culmination of an incredible journey that had begun with a simple idea back in Antarctica.

Over the following weeks and months, I developed strong relationships with the managers of all three markets - Damon, Jason, and Joe. One Wednesday market in September, towards the end of the day, I was enjoying a drink with Jason and Joe, when our conversation turned to plans for the end of December through February.

That's when I learned that due to Brisbane's hot, humid, and stormy summer weather, combined with school holidays, Christmas, New Year, and Australia Day at the end of January, the city tended to become very quiet. Most students went home, and many city workers took time off during this period, which meant that both city markets would shut down.

Having digested this information, I started thinking about how to handle the situation. I longed to find a project to occupy my mind, but the thought of committing to something long-term felt overwhelming. I had a blank canvas, and yet I couldn't seem to paint anything meaningful on it and my restlessness grew as I searched for something, anything, to fill the void of the markets during the summer.

The weight of unfulfilled potential hung heavy over me like an ominous storm cloud threatening to burst at any moment.

The Lottery

Across Australia, there are plenty of charitable lotteries that utilize their profits to offer assistance to those in need. This includes providing temporary housing to individuals without homes, funding important scientific research for cures to and treatments of life-threatening illnesses and offering aid to veterans and children.

My partner Michelle and I often found ourselves daydreaming about winning the grand prize and living a peaceful life in a charming countryside home. We have two beloved dogs and two cats who love to roam freely on vast green lawns, so we always make sure to attend open houses and try to envision ourselves in each one.

It's our little secret joke, hoping that someday our fortunes will shift, and we'll be the winners of the next draw. We always start with the kitchen, where Michelle checks if it's well-equipped for her own private chef—me!

Anyway, I was having lunch one day with "P", an old friend of mine, when he told me about a lottery being run to help out MS Queensland.

The first prize was usually a fancy car and since I was only the proud owner of a Renault Trafic Van for my pretzel business, winning one would be tremendous. He mentioned that the odds were much higher than other lotteries as there were only 8000 tickets at fifty dollars each. We discussed our thoughts on the chance of winning over some wine and although I wasn't claiming to be a statistician, in my opinion, it was like anything else in life - either you win, or you lose; the odds don't make a difference!

So, that day, I decided to take a chance and buy a ticket online. As I surfed the site, my attention was captured by the alternative reward if you didn't want the car: a visit to Antarctica. It excited me to imagine that I could go back one day, not as a chef this time, but as a tourist.

My mother always told me when I was young: "Sebastien, if you want something, you have to have faith in it!" So, I let my imagination wander and started picturing myself boarding the plane or the boat to Antarctica, surrounded once again by the breathtaking landscapes of glaciers and endless frozen wilderness and the cold crisp air. I thought about all the activities I could do there, such as visiting penguin colonies, ice climbing, and perhaps even making it to the South Pole?

I was almost becoming delusional as I lost myself in the daydream. I thought of being on board a cruise ship with Michelle, sipping champagne and looking out at the gargantuan icebergs. The idea of a trip to Antarctica was so compelling that I was nearly convinced that we were going to win it.

But then, reality kicked in and I reminded myself that winning any lottery requires a large amount of sheer luck. Nevertheless, I kept thinking positively – surely this time would be ours! I had faith in us both. Michelle is an incredibly gifted artist and I knew that if we won, she would be able to use the trip to create some beautiful works of art, inspired by nature's beauty. So, we waited for the big day when the winner would be announced.

On the day of the draw, we anxiously waited for the call that would tell us we had won, but of course, it never came! I felt completely defeated when I heard the news; I was so certain of victory that I had been able to close my eyes and vividly picture myself packing my bags.

It was a harsh reality to accept. I marched up to the rubbish bin and tossed the ticket inside, about to give up on my dream of returning to Antarctica for good. Suddenly, in a last-ditch effort to cling to hope, I fished the ticket back out of the bin and glanced at it. Little did I know then, but that simple action of retrieving the ticket would have life-altering consequences for me. The ticket was the size of a DL envelope with an image of the desolate Antarctic terrain in the background, and it said, "A trip to Antarctica". Was it a cruise? I remembered seeing an advertisement in the newspaper for a boat leaving from South America.

I scrutinised the bottom of the ticket and two words jumped out at me: WHITE DESERT.

It was the company sponsoring the trip. I quickly looked them up on the internet and navigated to their website. It turned out that White Desert was a British tour operator based in Cape Town, South Africa who conducted expeditions to Antarctica. It was also the only company to offer a commercial private jet service to the continent.

The business concept of White Desert instantly fascinated me.

The organization seemed determined to make the remarkable continent of Antarctica available to all, not just adventurers explorers, or scientists.

A maximum of 14 people on each trip would be flown from Cape Town to Wolf's Fang Runway in Queen Maud Land, Antarctica, via private planes. The journey would then end with passengers checking in at the luxurious Whichaway Camp. I thought to myself that it would be an incredible way to spend some very unique holidays, but as I considered the idea of booking a holiday, I had to face the fact that I had nowhere near enough money for it.

My spirits fell again as I once more envisioned the opportunity slipping away, when suddenly, a brilliant idea came to me: Why not email them and suggest that I work for them as a chef?

I immediately sent an email expressing my credentials - experience as a chef on a research station, and my current status as a small business owner selling Pretzels at the local farmer's market. I made sure to emphasize that I was always ready and available on short notice, should anything happen to the incumbent chef on ice. This might have seemed presumptuous, but it was entirely plausible in the extremes of Antarctica; in fact, one of our chefs had had an accident once and fractured his leg, which required a replacement.

I scheduled the email to be sent on a Monday afternoon to ensure that it would be the first thing my contact saw upon opening their inbox, when factoring in the time zone difference.

The following day, I was taken aback to receive a response from Katheryn, the F&B manager at the time. She inquired as to whether I would be available that week for a video call, and I found myself immediately filled with intense joy and elation. We settled on Thursday afternoon for our chat.

The day arrived in a heartbeat, and I was filled with a mix of excitement and apprehension as I started the video call with Katheryn. We discussed my experience as a chef, my current business venture, and what I would bring to White Desert should I be successful. She asked several engaging questions about food preferences, dietary restrictions awareness, and availability. Finally, she asked me how I had come to know about the job opening, since they had only just decided on that very Monday morning office meeting that they would hire a chef. I couldn't believe my luck!

She then asked if I would be interested in cooking for the staff at the runway, rather than the guests at the Whichaway camp. Would I be up for it?

My enthusiasm was palpable. My ambitions to return to Antarctica were finally coming true!

She then scheduled a video conference with Ags, the team leader at Wolf's Fang Runway. As soon as we started talking, I felt like I was having a chat with an old friend. Ags was a highly experienced Antarctic expeditioner who had been on several trips in the past with the British Antarctic Survey, including wintering on ice. She seemed like she had all the answers and knew every trick in the book when it came to surviving in such harsh conditions. As we talked, she explained the details of my job and what my daily duties would be. I would have to prepare meals for the staff at the runway, which would consist of around 10 people. The menu would vary every day, and I would have to work with limited ingredients, as everything had to be brought in by plane. She mentioned that the living situation at the runway was extremely simple, with only a few amenities. I don't recall this part of the conversation, but she also told me that we would each have a sleeping bag and an individual tent. We were to rely on one shared email address as our only method of communicating with the outside world. We'd have to take showers using a bucket and use a similarly primitive setup for the toilets.

But none of it phased me - I was far too excited about the prospect of returning to Antarctica and visiting an entirely new region. At the end of the conversation, she said cheerfully, *"Well Seb, it was nice to talk to you, see you on ice, bye for now!"*

Had I just been hired? Had there been some kind of misunderstanding between us? Or did she mean something else entirely?

After thinking for a while about my next step, I sent an email to Katheryn letting her know that the conversation with Ags had gone smoothly. Her response was immediate, and the next day she sent me a contract with all the details: dates, flight arrangements, itinerary, accommodation in Cape Town, transport from and to the airport - it was all there! I was elated; just like that, another job as a chef was in my hands. My heart was racing, and my enthusiasm knew no bounds. I couldn't believe the sheer luck of it; in a split second, my mood changed drastically, as if I were on an emotional rollercoaster.

After that initial elation, it suddenly hit me that my sister had already told me that she was going to come and visit Australia for Christmas and New Year, and that she had already bought tickets months ago to fly from France to Australia!

My heart sank. I couldn't believe it. The timing couldn't be worse! I had just landed another job in Antarctica, but my sister's visit was already set in stone.

I had to make a choice: go to Antarctica and miss spending the holidays with my sister or decline the job offer and spend the holidays with her.

It was a tough decision, so I emailed Katheryn and explained the situation.

The following day, as I was cooking dinner, my phone rang. It was Katheryn, calling from her office in Cape Town. I was worried about broaching the subject, but fortunately, she got straight to the point: there was someone else who could do the first part of the season, but they would need to be back in Cape Town by early January.

So, she offered me the opportunity to start on the 2nd of January, which coincided perfectly with my sister's date to return to France, which would be the 3rd.

I was delighted – it was the final piece of the puzzle!

Living and working on ice

My sister Marie, her husband Matthieu, and my nephew Louka had almost come to the end of their holiday. After a flight down from the Gold Coast to Sydney, we decided to stay in Manly for a few days and explore the city before New Year's Eve.

We had an amazing time exploring the city. The New Year's celebration was remarkable, particularly since I had dreamt of going since I was a kid. On national television, you could watch festivities from different countries around the world and I had always remembered Sydney's fireworks as being my favourite, so getting to see them in person was amazing.

The air in the city was alive with the energy of the New Year celebration. Everywhere you looked, people were wearing a variety of hats, streamers, and bright colours, shouting out their wishes for the upcoming year as the clock ticked closer to midnight. We were surrounded by a sea of strangers, but it felt like we were all connected in that moment, in a way that I couldn't explain. We stumbled up an alleyway behind the restaurant we'd had dinner at, and soon found ourselves under the harbor bridge.

The only way we could have been in a better spot would have been on one of the luxurious superyachts docked in the bay, but our wallets didn't quite stretch that far!

We watched in awe as the fireworks began to erupt from the bridge. The sky was lit up with a stunning display of lights, each one radiating an array of vivid reds, oranges, and blues that swirled and danced like a beautiful light show. We were enthralled; I had seen them on television, but in person, the entire experience was amplified. It was a sensory overload of colour, sound, and smell, all topped off with this intoxicating, electric feeling. The crowd cheered, clapped and hugged as the display of sparkling light grew ever more intense. It was an incredible way to begin the year, but the thought of going back to an even more remarkable place filled me with anticipation.

After a few hours of sleep, I'd take the memories we'd made that evening all the way to Cape Town, before heading back off to Antarctica.

The plane trip to South Africa passed so quickly, but I did my best to get as much sleep as I could. I knew that on arrival, I'd have to start working right away. I felt excited at the prospect of finally meeting Katheryn and finding out more about White Desert.

When I arrived, I was introduced to her at White Desert's office, where I also met another woman named Catherine. As someone who has trouble remembering names, this was pretty convenient. Katheryn "with a K" wasted no time in getting down to business.

She explained that White Desert was a luxury adventure travel company that specialised in taking clients on guided tours of one of the most inhospitable places on the planet, with two main focuses: reaching the South Pole and visiting a colony of Emperor penguins. By achieving these two things, White Desert was offering an experience unlike any other. She explained to me that the company had been founded by Patrick & Robyn, two extremely experienced polar expeditioners. For almost 20 years, they had been pioneering luxury tourism in Antarctica. She then informed me that Patrick usually came by the office in the middle of the day. I was both excited and somewhat daunted to finally meet the creator of the company in person. It almost felt like meeting a celebrity!

We then visited the warehouse, where people were busy packing various boxes of dried goods that would accompany me on my journey to Antarctica. This allowed me to get a better look at what was being transported to the icy continent. Katheryn was a pleasure to deal with. She had spent multiple years in Antarctica and had all the answers I needed. In my opinion, she is one of the most organised, patient, and skilful people I have ever come across, not to mention an excellent chef.

We would be working together during her tour of Antarctica, with several VIP guests staying over.

Our next stop was the production kitchen. She had already designed the menu, and multiple taste-testing sessions had been conducted to make sure we would be providing a top-notch feast for both our guests and our staff.

The process in the kitchen was similar to what you'd find in a typical restaurant: the chefs begin by doing their "mise en place"—the French term for prep work. This was the most crucial step, as it enabled us to be prepared for the lunch and dinner rush. We would portion out meat and fish, peel and chop vegetables, wash and cut lettuces and herbs, let stocks simmer, add last-minute touches to sauces, top up any necessary ingredients before service, and make sure there were enough plates and utensils. Also, we checked that the knives were sharp and ready for the service.

White Desert's process was much like in any other kitchen, except that the prep work was done in Cape Town and then everything would be shipped to Antarctica.

This approach reduced rubbish by eliminating unnecessary packaging and food waste, and since one of the conditions of being able to work in Antarctica was to leave it as pristine as you had found it, this was a major positive. Plus, with the limited equipment and cooking space, there truly wasn't much room for preparation on site anyway.

Of course, it was also crucial to double-check that all the necessary ingredients were there, as it wasn't like you could just run out to the local shop for a tub of butter if it was missing for the hollandaise sauce! The team responsible for organizing the "mise en place" had offered up a commendable effort - all the ingredients seemed to be present and accounted for, and I anticipated them coming with me to Antarctica in just a day or two (weather dependent), a process that would repeat itself with each rotation of planes during the season.

My responsibility now was to ensure that everyone involved felt happy, satisfied, and well-cared for. In the late afternoon, we went back to the office, and I got my clothing for the season, which had a sleeping bag included. I took this opportunity to inquire about the living arrangements once we arrived in Antarctica - something I hadn't thought of before. This was when Katheryn informed me about the showers and the email. The latter in particular felt like a scene from a sitcom, as I imagined myself mistakenly reading someone else's private message to their partner, or accidentally sending an intimate love letter to their long-distance girlfriend for everyone to read). It would be an embarrassing situation, but then again, perhaps I could turn it into a funny anecdote someday.

Either way, Katheryn's assurances that I would be fine eased my doubts; she had been to Antarctica multiple times and was an experienced chef and expeditioner. My excitement began to build as I imagined the different scenarios and experiences I'd have, compared with the comfort and luxury of a warm national Antarctic station. It felt like I was getting closer to what the original explorers had gone through.

Katheryn could hear Patrick and Robyn in the distance and excitedly announced, *"That's them! Let me introduce you!"*

I recall that day vividly. Even though I'm usually very comfortable around people, I felt a bit anxious partly due to their accomplishments, and partly because they were the owners of White Desert.

However, any apprehension was quickly extinguished when I met them both. They radiated joyfulness and energy, and immediately made me feel welcome and included. I'd say without a doubt that they were two of the most charismatic people I'd ever met.

As we chatted, I couldn't help but feel a sense of awe at their accomplishments. Patrick had traversed Antarctica, a feat that few people in the world had ever accomplished. Robyn, meanwhile, had skied to the North Pole, another incredible achievement. Yet despite their incredible achievements, they remained humble and down to earth, and more than happy to chat and share their knowledge and experiences with me.

I had been in Cape Town for less than a day, but as it turned out, I would not get much of a chance to visit the city as it was later confirmed that the weather in Antarctica was good enough to fly the next morning. I would board a plane with 11 Russian guests, all bound for a week's holiday at Whichaway camp in Antarctica. We headed to the hotel where the guests were staying. There, Patrick would greet them, present a safety briefing, provide them with polar gear, and inform us that there would be an early departure.

Our trip demanded that we take off at 6 am to avoid any weather surprises in Antarctica, so we had to make sure that we reached Cape Town International Airport by 4 am. We arrived at the hotel where the guests were staying at 7 pm, and the meeting and briefing took around an hour.

My day had already been hectic, but it was still far from over.

I smiled to myself as I recalled the conversations with friends back home in Australia who had asked me what I would be doing during my summer down south. I had simply replied that it was a working holiday, but in truth, it was far more the former than the latter.

It was getting close to nine in the evening when Katheryn and I reached our lodging for the night.

Although we were famished, neither of us had the motivation to prepare dinner, so we just sat down with a beer and ordered some takeaway food on Uber Eats instead. As we ate, we caught each other's eye and laughed; two highly qualified chefs, reduced to such a state!

I woke up early the following morning, eager to have a hot shower and shave before leaving. I wasn't sure when I would have access to basic amenities again, so I wanted to take the opportunity while I still had it. This was going to be a new challenge for me: typically, I'd never gone more than three days without shaving and my hair had been short or shaved for as long as I could remember. I'm usually more of a Kelly Slater than a Zach Galifianakis!

Katheryn drove me to the international airport, where other Catherine was waiting to pick me up. I had encountered her briefly the morning before and had learned enough to know that she held a few different positions within White Desert and was highly involved with Patrick and Robyn's business.

We quickly passed through passport control with our VIP status and were almost immediately taken away from the main area in a car and dropped off in front of the Gulfstream 550 private jet.

It was well before sunrise and the event felt very mysterious, almost like being in an action movie. The sky was still dark, and the runway was lit with two rows of lights, with a few other jets parked nearby. There was a scent of aviation fuel in the air. It was familiar from my frequent flights, and at this point, even almost comforting.

The excitement reached fever pitch when the eleven Russian men arrived. I couldn't help but feel a bit intimidated as they towered over me with their stern, stoic expressions. Even though they had spread out across the globe in their adulthood, these friends had now found themselves together again, ready to embark on an adventure to the most secluded spot on the planet.

Katheryn was in the middle of a lengthy discussion with the pilot, as we had more cargo than would fit on the plane.

But after some efficient negotiating and a little bit of re-packing, she eventually persuaded him to let us take off. We were all ready for departure!

I felt a mixture of emotions as we said goodbye to Katheryn and Cape Town; it would be a few months before we returned from Antarctica. Although I'd only been there for just a day, I already felt incredibly connected to the city, but I couldn't put my finger on why. It wouldn't be until my return that I finally understood the mysterious bond between myself and this place.

It was the start of an adventure that would change my life! After take-off, the Russian men seemed to be just as excited as I was, chatting and laughing together in their native tongue, playing poker and drinking vodka of course! I couldn't understand a word they were saying, but their infectious energy was enough to make me smile.

The flight from Cape Town to Wolf's Fang Runway was set to last five hours, but the excitement kept me on edge the entire time. I felt like a celebrity surrounded by such luxury - I had never flown outside of economy class before. The soft, tan-leather seats on the jet were exquisite, each one upholstered by hand with a precision that could only have come from meticulous craftsmanship. Polished wood panelling and crown moulding fit in with the colour scheme of light browns, making it feel like you were in some sort of living room, rather than 30,000 feet in the air. It was a far cry from the cramped, uncomfortable commercial flights I was used to.

The plane soared over the vast expanse of the Southern Ocean, and as I stared out the window, a sense of awe washed over me at the sheer scale of the world. The ocean stretched for miles in every direction, an endless expanse of blue that merged with the horizon in a seamless blend. It was as if we were gliding through a painting, one where brushstrokes of turquoise and azure met in a kaleidoscope of colours.

The sky above was pale white and baby blue, dotted with wispy clouds that trailed behind us like tendrils of smoke. As we flew further over the horizon, it seemed like there was no end to this breathtaking view. The guests were wondering why I was there, so I began to tell them about my previous expedition to Antarctica. They could all speak English fluently and it was easy to tell by the way they talked, the clothes they wore and, most importantly, the fact that everyone was wearing Rolex watches (not fakes!) that this was a group of wealthy individuals with important jobs or occupations. This didn't come as a shock, as travelling to Antarctica wasn't a cheap voyage for the average working-class man.

Four-and-a-half hours into the flight, we were instructed to put on our polar gear in preparation for landing in Antarctica. For the final thirty minutes of the journey, the plane's temperature was dropped to reduce the difference between inside and outside when we disembarked.

We were on the final descent towards Wolf's Fang Runway in Queen Maud Land; I could see the daunting Ulvetanna Peak (2930m) off in the distance. Once we touched down, the 11 Russian guests boarded a DC3 airplane for a 20-minute flight to their final destination: the Whichaway camp.

The luxury flagship of White Desert sits on the shores of one of the freshwater lakes of Schirmacher Oasis on Princess Astrid Coast, in Queen Maud's Land.

The landing strip was made of special, expertly crafted blue ice, making it one of the most comfortable landings that I'd ever experienced. The snow-covered mountains surrounding the runway had a majestic beauty to them, the glistening white cascading down the slopes as if it were a blanket of untouched perfection.

As soon as the plane's wheels touched down on the ice, I knew that I was in for a completely different experience than my previous trip to Antarctica.

The Russian men were already jumping out of their seats, grabbing their bags and polar gear, and shuffling towards the exit. I followed suit, making sure that I had all of my essentials with me.

Outside, the sky was a brilliant blue and clear above us, giving way to an unobstructed view for miles in every direction. The air was crisp and cold, yet surprisingly refreshing. It was so quiet that it almost seemed like time itself had stood still. I could hear nothing but my breath, and I felt the pure silence that surrounded me.

This place had an aura of mystery and wonderment that I couldn't quite put into words. It was almost like coming home after being away for too long, a feeling of nostalgia mixed with intrigue drawing me further into this mysterious continent.

When I disembarked from the plane, Ags was there to meet me. We had only spoken before via video call, so it felt great to finally meet her in person. We had no time for a lengthy chat, though, as she was busy with the plane.

She informed me that the 11 Russian guests wouldn't be able to leave right away because the weather at Whichaway wasn't good, and then, while expressing her regret for putting me in this position, she explained that this meant I would have to make lunch. She motioned towards a distant tent and said I could find the kitchen there, then apologised again, this time for not being able to take me around as she had to remain by the plane.

Not wanting to worry her, I assured her I could handle it myself. As I was walking towards the large Alaskan tent in the distance, (a kind of robust shelter designed to withstand the freezing, windy conditions of Antarctica) the atmosphere reminded me of my days as a fly-in, fly-out chef in the Australian mines.

I had worked that job for years, so I was used to jumping right into action and taking on all new challenges without fear. I remembered for a second what my friend Colin used to say: "It is what it is, Sebbie!"

The current situation was no different. As I approached the tent, I could make out a mini campsite on ice. I realised that this would be my home for the next couple of months, but I remained unfazed. Instead of stressing about sleeping in a nylon tent, I had to focus on preparing lunch for the 11 Russian men and the staff. I entered the tent from the northern side.

My first step across the threshold would lead me to a small area that was similar to the "cold porch" on the station, but much smaller. The room was roughly four metres by one metre, acting as a vestibule for the team members to take off their outer layers and gloves before entering for meals or rest. This area was also the designated spot for storing cold food. As there was no refrigerator available, it was the perfect location due to the temperature of the vestibule, which hovered just above freezing point. The frozen goods would have to be left outside, nestled beneath a thick layer of snow that served as both a natural freezer and a refuge from the sun. Any perishable items were carefully placed in the makeshift snow cooler, ensuring they would stay fresh for as long as possible. It was a delicate balance between protecting the food and preserving its quality, one that had to be constantly monitored in such a harsh climate with limited infrastructure and equipment.

After moving through the second door, I arrived at what served as both the kitchen and gathering place for the staff to get meals and spend time in.

The space was small, about 4 metres by 4 metres. On my right side, there was a small bench made of two trestles topped with a piece of wood, an old gas stove and oven, and another identical bench. In the corner of the room sat a circular cast-iron fireplace with a kettle resting atop it. On the left side of the kitchen was a wall of shelves with all sorts of miscellaneous items, including everyone's toiletry kits. They were largely in there because otherwise, when temperatures in the sleeping tent got below zero degrees, toothpaste would freeze solid! There was a table with eight camping chairs, a tiny sink, two blue barrels underneath to catch grey water, and another bench similar to the ones on the other side of the kitchen. On the bench was a large metal tank filled with clean water, and another blue barrel below it for dirty water. This would be the system for washing our hands and brushing our teeth. The rays of the sun beamed through the side windows, casting a comforting light throughout the room.

I had an incredible view over Ulvetanna Peak straight ahead of me – it was like being transported to another era; this kitchen was so different from what I was used to. Even though it felt as if everything had been preserved in time, the view made up for any other deficiencies! I took a deep breath and got to work, rifling through the food supplies to see what ingredients I had to work with. I also knew what we had with us on the plane and was expecting that food to appear at any moment.

I gathered pasta, a selection of root vegetables, some bacon, and a few different spices and decided to make a vegetable soup with garlic bread and pasta carbonara. The cold weather made me certain the soup would be popular. A carbonara was an easy meal that could be prepared quickly, while the fresh food from the plane provided the perfect ingredients for a fruit platter for dessert. I diced the vegetables for the soup quickly and skilfully and sautéed the bacon and onions for the carbonara while the spaghetti boiled away. In this tiny kitchen filled with delicious aromas and noises of cooking, I felt oddly at ease.

The meal was prepared quickly, and they all enjoyed the simple yet delicious food. I served it without any fancy plating up, instead placing it in the middle of the table for them to share. The soup was warm and comforting, full of hearty root vegetables and fragrant spices.

The carbonara was creamy and flavourful, with the bacon adding a smoky richness. The fruit platter was fresh and juicy, providing a light, refreshing finish to the meal. And yes, as I had predicted, the soup was indeed an excellent choice - every drop of it was gone! I could hear the jet engines start up, so I went outside to watch the plane take off.

There was something special about it; maybe it was the fact that we were on a runway on blue ice, or perhaps it was the sound of the loud engine as it catapulted itself upward into the clear blue sky, or even because I knew that its passengers would be back in civilization tonight?

Whatever the reason, though, one thing is still certain to this day: I never tire of watching planes take off and land. There's just something unique about it!

Ags and her cohort shambled towards the staff mess tent, a place where individuals congregated to consume large quantities of food like military personnel on an army base. She stood in front of everyone and virtually dragged me alongside her, then introduced me as the fantastic chef who could make 11 Russian guests and 12 starving Antarctic ground crew lunch in less than 60 minutes. It wasn't rocket science: all I had to do was transform the same dish I had already prepared to feed twice as many people. But you only get one shot at making a good first impression, and I thought that I had nailed it!

Just after lunchtime, we received a transmission from the Whichaway camp informing us that the skyway up on the plateau had cleared and they were ready to receive our 11 Russian visitors. I bid them farewell, wishing them a great trip and holidays. I told them that we would see each other again when they returned to Cape Town the following week.

As we watched the plane take off, my bladder desperately reminded me that I had to use the toilet. When I asked John, the medic, where they were located, he pointed toward a blue Weatherheaven tent in the distance and said, *"Do you know how to use a Pacto?"*

I had no idea what one was, so we journeyed towards it together, me feeling like an imbecile who had to be shown how to use a toilet at the age of 47!

He informed me that there was a blue drum for urine and the Pacto was for "number 2s" only.

Apparently, peeing in it was a bad idea because if the liner ripped during the emptying process, it would result in a much messier disaster. When I was done, I was to press the pedal to flush, causing the waste to move into an internal container. A new liner would be supplied automatically, and a mechanical seal would activate to keep any odours away. I was impressed by the technology.

"But what happens with the waste?" I asked him.

He replied, *"We have a schedule for Pacto duties. One of us is assigned to empty the base and refill the liners when needed. The waste is stored in sealed drums and taken back to Cape Town for proper disposal. Fortunately for you, we all decided that the chef shouldn't be on duty for this job - it's not exactly the most pleasant idea to have him handling other people's waste."*

I smiled internally, relieved to hear of my good fortune!

As I took my first steps towards my new home, a small yellow nylon tent, I could feel the chill in the air. Kneeling beside it, I unzipped the flap and peered inside. It was sparsely furnished with black foam insulation lining the floor and a single inflatable mattress at the top. No frills or fuss!

I was relieved to have been given a polar-graded sleeping bag in Cape Town before beginning the journey; without it, I would have had no respite from the ice-cold interior of the tent. But even with its protection, I couldn't help but shiver as I imagined spending numerous nights in such a cramped space. It was going to be a big part of my life over the next few years - sleeping on ice in a small tent.

It was still early January, but I had already made it to the little yellow dwelling I'd been dreaming of for weeks. The sun shone brightly during that time of year and never set, but although the idea of 24-hour daylight seemed exciting at first, I soon found that its constant presence was to have an adverse effect on my already frayed circadian rhythm.

My first night in the tent was much warmer than anticipated; the bright yellow canvas seemed to attract and absorb the sunlight, making it a bit too hot and stuffy inside. So, for the next few nights, I decided to keep my zipper open with the hope of letting some fresh air circulate through. I was thankful to have brought along my airline vanity bag which contained an eye mask, blocking out the intense brightness that would otherwise have kept me up all night long. In the morning, though, it meant I would stumble out of my small tent and into the blinding light, my eyes squeezed shut in protest.

I quickly realised the necessity of wearing sunglasses whenever I did this, as the reflection on the ice, combined with the clear sky, made it even brighter than usual.

On arrival at the mess tent, I would immediately put a pot of coffee on the camping stove. During this time, I would also usually do my daily 'Antarctic workout' outside.

On the left side of the tent was a huge stainless-steel container which served as our ice melter. My first task was the laborious job of breaking up chunks of snow and ice and shovelling them into the melter, which could take hours to melt down enough water for us to use during the day. Once this was done, the liquid was brought into the mess tent and stored in the second stainless steel tank, atop a trestle table next to the sink.

Just as I had finished these tasks, John arrived. He was an early riser and over the coming weeks and months, we both took part in this same ritual together. It was a routine that had to be completed at least three times a day to make sure we had enough water. But hey - who needed a gym?

The day before had been hectic, especially since the eleven Russian guests had had to wait for the weather to clear up. We would only host customers at the Runway in worst-case scenarios, such as if trips were cancelled by bad conditions, but normally, my job was far more straightforward and predictable.

The fact that we could take our guests to the South Pole without having to walk like Patrick and other super-fit adventurers did, was a massive draw due to the DC3 Basler aircrafts at the runway.

That season, we were able to have two planes stationed at Wolf's Fang, each consisting of two pilots and one mechanic. The planes had made a remarkable voyage all the way from Oshawa, Canada. Just before lunchtime, I met Brian, Ronda, Cullen and Mac who were in one plane while John, Rick, and Joe had come in on another.

All of them hailed from Canada. Ronda recounted to me the whirlwind of activity that had happened between the lead-up and their launch in early October, which was a flurry of completing airplane-related activities, packing supplies, and training. It was hard to ship things to the camp, so they had to prepare carefully and make sure they only brought the absolute necessities.

Brian had a great level of expertise, having spent over two decades on ice. Ronda brought a touch of luxury and comfort to the aircrew stationed in Antarctica, raising their living standards and providing an oasis amidst the harsh terrain. As for Cullen, he was your typical "happy-go-lucky" dude and a breeze to get along with - oh, and his piloting skills were second to none!

On the initial day of their journey, they left Oshawa and flew to Nassau in the Bahamas. Arriving earlier than expected, they had taken a quick dip in the water before heading over to the fish fry for supper. There, they had found some of the best, most authentic Bahamian cuisine around. Ronda was always raving about how tasty it was!

The crew had stopped for fuel in Panama before heading to Arica, Chile, where they would always celebrate with a special cocktail. With her appreciation of good food, drinks, and company, it was understandable why Ronda was regarded as the most valuable person in the aviation team.

On day three, the plan had been to travel either to La Serena or Concepcion in Chile, depending on the climate and intensity of any forest fires. Then, on day four, they had finally arrived in Punta Arenas, Chile, the last leg of their journey to Antarctica.

Ryan flew in from New Zealand and was assigned to manage the setup and running of the airstrip, Jean Seb came from France and was renowned for being one of the top snow groomers in the world, and Oleg had made the journey from Cape Town to provide comms expertise alongside Skipper, who was in charge of the traverse team. Together, they would all proceed to fly across to Antarctica to open the camp and prepare the runway for the incoming jet, which would be bringing additional team members for the season within a few weeks.

The aviation team modified the plane by adding ski attachments so they could land on snow or ice-covered surfaces during their missions. This process took an entire day, and when the skies cleared, they were ready to take flight over the Drake Passage towards Rothera Station, which was managed by the British Antarctic Survey.

That's where their mission would begin. In the past, they had found themselves waiting up to a week for suitable weather conditions, but Punta was secure place with good food, according to the all-knowing Ronda. Julio, their handler, assisted them in getting all of the last-minute supplies for the season.

From Rothera, the team's next stop was Wolf's Fang Runway. But, depending on the weather at their destination, they sometimes had to stay at Neumayer, the German Antarctic research station, for a few days to wait for better conditions before flying to Wolfs Fang.

Ronda mentioned that it was always exciting to land at Wolf's Fang and experience that feeling of there being just snow and ice for miles, with nobody else around. After hearing the tale, I felt safe for our future trips, knowing the pilots were so experienced with that kind of landing.

The descent had been smooth, and luckily there wasn't too much snow accumulated on the ground, so they were able to start unloading faster than usual. Some years, they would have to spend hours shovelling before they could even access the equipment that was stored in shipping containers during winter, resulting in them needing to pitch a tent for the night.

The cold air seemed to energize the team, who moved with speed and purpose. Even though it was late October when they arrived, the chill of winter still lingered in the air. The sun had already sunk beneath the horizon, leaving the sky an inky black, punctured only by the occasional bright stars.

Ryan and Jean Seb ploughed around the perimeter of the camp, clearing out the snow, then starting to work on creating a runway.

Oleg was busy getting the communication system running while Skipper worked on the machinery. Everyone helped with setting up the camp and shovelling away any snow that had accumulated during the months-long darkness of winter, trying to make sure everything was as it should be. Ronda started melting some ice for water and preparing food from a cache that had been left from the previous season.

After dinner, everyone was exhausted and eagerly collapsed into their tents for much-needed rest. In the coming weeks, more crew members from White Desert would join us in the remote location, but a feeling of camaraderie had already settled in. Everyone enjoyed working together and taking on new challenges.

After months of meticulous planning, the first flight arrived carrying Luke from Durban in South Africa who was appointed to oversee Atka Bay camp and take the guests on a day trip to the Emperor penguin colony. There was also Manu, the head mountain guide, who had come from the French Alps to manage the guides and organize all sorts of activities such as hikes for all levels of fitness, ice or rock climbing, mountain biking on ice, walking through some beautiful ice tunnels, or exploring the ice caves with their stunning deep blue ice crystals. The plane also held personnel who would open and oversee Whichaway camp: a camp manager, front-of-house manager, chef, jack-of-all-trades handyman, mechanic/driver, doctor, general handyperson, two camp assistants, and three mountain guides. The twelve of them would combine their efforts to give the season's visitors the ultimate luxurious experience. Their mission was to open up the winterised camp before the next plane with passengers arrived, and make sure that everything was in good working order.

The task I had at Wolf's Fang Runway was less complicated than that of Anthony (Ant), the chef at Whichaway. There were no guests to cook for, but I still considered the Wolf's Fang Runway staff as paying customers, and I wanted to ensure that their satisfaction was top priority. After all, we would be stuck in the same place for a long time with no other food options around. Whenever they would rave about the food, I would joke by saying, "Don't forget to give us a good review on TripAdvisor! It's a small business and we need all the positive feedback we can get!" From prior expeditions, I knew even something as simple as freshly baked bread could bring joy, so I made sure there was some available every day.

Oleg always seemed to have an uncanny sense of timing - he would magically appear in the kitchen tent right when I took the warm bread out of the oven!

Occasionally, three Russians would make their way to the camp to resupply their food before they continued their traverse. I kindly nicknamed them the truckies of Antarctica, but they were much more than that; they were essential to the success of our entire operation. Skipper, Vlad, and Andrei made up the traverse team. They were unbelievably experienced, very proficient, and incredibly resilient expeditioners who had been coming to Antarctica for decades. Most of them endured winter on one of the Russian stations for eighteen to twenty-four months with barely any convenience or connection to the outside world. They were also all notorious outlaws on the most wanted list from Interpol and Scotland Yard... or that's what they'd have you think. In reality, they were the meekest, most talented, quietest folk I knew, and they had loving families eagerly anticipating their return. The traverse team had been appointed to retrieve the cargo and fuel from "the depot" after it had been delivered by the South African icebreaker S.A Agulhas II. This was after it had already taken another journey of 4280 km from Cape Town to the Ekström Ice Shelf next to the South African National Antarctic Expedition (SANAE) research station.

That year, Carl was in charge of the depot. He was a larger- than-life South African guy with an infectious smile and a boisterous laugh no matter what kind of predicament he was in. It was that self-assured outlook that was useful for him as he faced the obstacles that would arise in the coming season. The traverse team launched out of Wolf's Fang Runway on an 800 km course across some of Earth's most dangerous landscapes.

They travelled in a PistenBully, a snow groomer made to withstand the most extreme conditions, travelling at speeds of up to 10 kilometres per hour for as long as it took (hopefully no more than 6 to 8 days), using ice-penetrating radar, ensuring that they avoided any hidden crevasses that may pose a risk. After reaching their destination, they then set off on another 800km route back to Wolfs Fang, where some of the cargo was unloaded. From there, they then continued on a 1300 km mission toward Dixie to replenish fuel and collect the supplies that would be necessary for the planes taking clients to the South Pole.

Three Russian men, Dimitri, Pavel, and Andrei were taking care of the camp that season to make sure it was ready for the guests' arrival. They also assisted the pilots and plane mechanics to ensure a smooth re-fuelling process.

Patrick and Robyn, long-time friends of Dirk "Dixie" Dansercoer, had lovingly named the camp in his memory. He died on 7 June 2021 during an expedition in Greenland at the age of 58, having gone missing after falling into a glacier gorge. It is unclear if his body will ever be recovered. A search and rescue team was able to descend into the crevasse and locate his sled at a depth of 25 m, but was unable to find him after descending a further 15 m. No further rescue attempts were undertaken. Dansercoer recorded in his last journal entry, 443 km from the destination Qaanaaq: "nice temperatures, terrain wonderful and perfect visibility". According to his expedition partner, Sebastien Audy, Dansercoer was man-hauling the sled when the accident occurred.

I had the chance to meet Dixie a couple of years before the accident, he was a truly high-achieving and skilled explorer yet a very humble and joyful individual. Life on the runway was great; we all got along with one another as like-minded individuals. Every day, someone had to perform at least one (or sometimes two) grey water runs - taking the water from the blue drums under the kitchen sink and the pee drums, and manually emptying them since there was no sewage system in place at our temporary camp.

In the kitchen, Felix from Quebec and Jean Seb from France were always willing to lend a helping hand with the dishes. Our conversations were filled with laughter, and I fondly nicknamed them "cassos" and "charette" respectively.

Felix was used to the cold, so working as a mechanic in Antarctica presented no real issue to him. I remember on a windy day, he actually came to me and said his fingers were numb with cold. When I asked if he needed any help getting warm again, he answered in the affirmative, so I jokingly suggested washing some dishes, explaining that in no time at all, his hands would be nice and toasty!

It was a great relief to be disconnected from the outside world, not having to worry about what was happening beyond our group, and not being exposed to all the advertising, gossip, news, politics, scandals, or criminal activity. All that mattered here was having fun and enjoying ourselves!

John had spent almost 30 years flying a DC-3. He had a way of transporting the entire group to another world every time he told a story. He'd even sit up straight in his seat, adjust the old leather straps around him, pull down on the brim of his cap, and squint as if he were looking out into the sky. His stories would bring us along for the full journey, from taking off at LaGuardia to touching down in Cuba or Albuquerque.

We all knew he was special; his gift was taking people back in time through his tales. I remember sitting in the mess, my laptop open on the table as I scrolled through a series of photographs. John was sitting beside me, his hands wrapped around his steaming mug of coffee, when he suddenly leaned in and pointed to an image of a DC3 with a Chinese flag painted on its tail.

The airplane appeared blazing red against the pristine snow-covered backdrop below, with a penguin colony in the foreground. Its wingspan looked minuscule compared to the towering icebergs that stood to each side.

His voice rippled with enthusiasm as he inquired, *"Where did you take this shot? Where is this place?"* I told him that I had been at Davis Station, run by the Australian Antarctic Division, a few years before. The plane had just returned from Casey Station after dropping off some scientists who were done with their research project.

He proclaimed that he recognised me, as had been the pilot of the plane and had had to stay at Davis for the night. I asked him if he was experiencing "Déja vu," and we both laughed at the incredibly unlikely coincidence.

Acclimatising to my new living circumstances was not without its hiccups. I had become accustomed to sleeping in the nylon tent and going without social media, and I found that playing cards with my fellow explorers was a great way to pass the time. However, I hadn't accounted for the difficulty of taking a shower. Generally, it can be quite an ordeal to get clean while living at the Runway; first, you would have to melt the ice, then warm up the water, make sure no one is around when you go to take a "bucket" shower, grab your clothing from the other tent...the whole process would sometimes take me more than an hour. But as I soon found out, two major difficulties made this task even more of a struggle: The first time, I misjudged the water temperature. I thought it was hot enough, only to realize that it was far warmer on my skin than when I had tested it with my hand (which ended up being painful), and the winds were particularly strong that day, and the tent was filled with gaps. As such, I quickly went from steaming hot to freezing cold while taking a shower. What had started as an underwhelming attempt at getting clean, ended up becoming a complete failure. I got used to just using wet wipes to clean myself, as others before and after me had always done. The good thing about Antarctica is that the cold temperatures and lack of humidity result in very little sweat or body odour.

Washing clothes was another tricky problem. Since it was either too hot or too cold for proper washing, drying them also posed a challenge. We resorted to hanging our clothes up inside our tent when the sun was out, which helped dry them quickly. Other times, we would hang them up outside and leave them for a few hours; this process essentially freeze-dried the garments! We were content with the results, at least until we arrived in Cape Town a couple of weeks later. But that's a story for later!

Time flew by at an incredible speed, perhaps because I was used to being on ice for longer periods in previous seasons, or perhaps because the runway was always buzzing with activity.

Jets came and went every week, bringing new people to experience the wonder of the icy land around us, and taking away those who had basked in its glory for too long.

In between arrivals and departures, the aviation team would take guests to see the penguin colony at Atka Bay or accompany them on a once-in-a-lifetime trip to the South Pole. If they weren't doing that, they were busy with fuel runs between the depot and the runway. By the beginning of February, the last group of visitors had left, and our team was tasked with getting everything ready for winter.

We had to take apart each field camp; Dixie, Atka Bay, and the depot and store all of the equipment, gear, trash, cardboard, and recycling glass and human waste in secure containers. All of it was then taken on a traverse to Agulhas and properly disposed of in Cape Town.

On the second-to-last flight, Patrick and Ben showed up unexpectedly. They were doing research for their next endeavours, but they were also there to lend a hand when it came time to wrap things up. We were all pleased with their help, and their presence just showed how good the feeling of teamwork was over there. Over a period of four days, our team of thirteen worked diligently until everything was packed and ready to go.

Finally, the day had come: the jet would make its last trip into Antarctica to bring us back home to Cape Town. The landscape when we first arrived had been wide open and pristine, with untouched snow-covered land and ice stretching for miles. As we prepared to leave, it was just as untouched as before; everything from the tents to the equipment was packed away carefully and securely, meaning that the only evidence of our presence would be the footprints in the snow (which would soon be covered once more) and the memories we would take with us.

The Canadian aviation team, who had been first to arrive, was also the last to depart, waiting to make sure that the jet had taken off and was safely soaring through the air. It was a bittersweet moment to bid farewell to all of them.

We all boarded the jet with a mixture of joy and sorrow, looking forward to simple things like taking a real bath, using a proper toilet, sleeping in an actual bed, and not having to wiggle into our clothes like centipedes when getting dressed. I was especially excited for the first cooked meal in months that I hadn't had to prepare myself.

The engines began to roar more and more loudly as the jet slowly made its way on the runway, gathering speed until we shot off into the sunny blue sky like an arrow. We could hear the sound of each engine revving up, the pitch going higher and higher as they worked together to lift us from the surface of Antarctica.

The force of their thrust kept us pinned to our seats as we climbed until we were eventually gliding effortlessly over the vast white landscape below. The pilot then switched direction, heading due north towards Cape Town. The sunlight came streaming through my window, and all I could make out far below us were the two DC3s about to take off. Nothing else! We had left without a trace, and it was an inspiring sight! Though life on that isolated continent had been tough, all the memories that I had created there brought me such joy, and one thing was certain: I would be back.

Cape Town

The journey from Wolf's Fang Runway to Cape Town was one to remember. As soon as we had taken off, we began celebrating the end of a successful season in true style.

The atmosphere was euphoric, our very own VIP party soaring through the skies above the Antarctic Ocean.

It had been a long time since we had experienced total darkness, and it added an eerie element to the festivities.

Once we had landed in Cape Town and walked through the VIP terminal, we noticed that the airport seemed deserted. This turned out to be a blessing, as our group was quite a sight to behold, with one member in particularly rough shape. We ended up having to push him on a luggage trolley to get through the terminal.

As we made our way towards the exit, I could see Catherine and Katheryn in the distance. They didn't seem too impressed by our state, but they handled it gracefully and arranged for a shuttle bus to take us to our hotel in downtown Cape Town, which was a relief after such a chaotic journey. It had been heartwarming to have someone waiting for us at such a late hour, but that's just how caring and thoughtful those two ladies were. They truly wanted us all to make it back safely.

It was now 11:30 pm and I had finally made it into my hotel room. I was excited about my time in Cape Town particularly because, in the past, I had always left Antarctica through Hobart, Australia when I was with the AAD. This trip would allow me to experience a new city and all it had to offer.

The first thing I did was take a brief look around, open the sliding door of my balcony, and step outside into the mild and pleasant night. Although it was too dark to see the ocean, I could smell its salty mist gently enveloping my skin. As I turned to go back inside, I almost tripped over my duffle bag, which contained all my Antarctic gear. Since I didn't need it anymore, having packed my clothes for my stay in

Cape Town in a separate backpack, I decided to move it out onto the balcony for some extra space.

I sat down and grabbed the phone next to my bed to call room service. After three months of dreaming about this moment, I ordered a bottle of Sauvignon Blanc and prepared for a relaxing bath despite the late hour. While waiting for the wine to arrive, I ran the bath and emptied the whole bottle of shampoo into it, creating an alarming amount of bubbles. After living in harsh conditions for months, this small indulgence felt like pure magic.

The next morning, I woke up at 6:30 am to a gentle light seeping through the curtains and a white ceiling above me. It took a few moments for my brain to register that I was in a hotel room in Cape Town, a stark contrast to the past 50 days spent sleeping in a small tent on ice. As I sat up on the edge of the queen-sized bed, my feet almost brushing against the floor, I couldn't help but feel overwhelmed by the sudden luxury and convenience. There was no more scavenging for semi-clean clothes, no more wiggling into them while laying flat inside the tent. No need anymore to get dressed and trek through the wilderness just to use a toilet. Once again, I could enjoy the simple pleasure of running water. It was something we had obviously taken for granted all our lives, but the memory had been eroded during our time in Antarctica. Now, in the blink of an eye, it was all easily accessible once more. The last few days in Antarctica had been physically and mentally taxing as we packed up our camps and battled constant winds and plummeting temperatures.

But on that day, as I woke up, I had no deadlines or worries besides taking care of myself. After noticing a kettle and coffee selection by the mini bar fridge, I indulged in a hot cup of coffee before heading for a refreshing shower. As I stepped out, I poured myself another cup of coffee and decided to sit outside on the balcony and watch the city come to life.

The bustling streets were filled with people, hurrying to start their day. The air carried the scent of freshly brewed coffee from nearby cafes, mixed with the sweet fragrances of blooming flowers and the salty breeze from the ocean. There was also a faint hint of exhaust fumes from the passing cars, trucks, and minibuses honking and weaving their way through the streets, accompanied by the constant noise of whistling as people tried to attract attention. It was quite a change from the peaceful mornings in Antarctica. Suddenly, I heard a buzzing sound near me, which caught me off guard.

I looked around and noticed it was coming from my duffel bag, which I had left on the balcony overnight. I unzipped it and rummaged through until I found my mobile phone. The buzzing noise turned out to be a Skype call from my mother in France.

I picked up the phone and greeted her, *"Hi mum, how are you?"*

"How are you doing? Did you make it out of Antarctica? Where are you now?" she asked.

"I'm okay. I just woke up after arriving late last night in South Africa. I'll be here for about a week before flying back to Australia."

"What do you mean you're in South Africa? Weren't you working in Antarctica?" she asked, confused.

It suddenly occurred to me that I had forgotten to tell her about my new job with White Desert, which was based in Cape Town, South Africa. After explaining everything to her, I could hear the excitement in her voice shift as she started telling me stories about her father's time in Cape Town during World War II.

At that very moment, I realised that I would finally uncover the reason behind the mysterious connection I had felt with the place since my brief stop three months ago.

My grandfather's story had gone like this:

During WWII, he served as an electro-mechanic on a French submarine stationed in the Indian Ocean near the island of Diego-Suarez. They had been given orders to make contact with a ship that was travelling down the West coast of Africa to deliver supplies to Madagascar for military and civilians.

The mission was to wait for the ship at a designated point off the coast of Durban, South Africa (lat.30°S), and escort it back to Madagascar.

After waiting for over a week without success, they were redirected further south to Port Elizabeth (lat.33°S). But again, after another week of failed attempts at contacting the ship, they were ordered to head even further south to the Cape of Good Hope (lat.34°S), which was the furthest point they were allowed to go.

Finally, they made contact with the ship and agreed to wait for it to reach them, but their transmission was intercepted by the enemy and a fierce battle ensued. The ship was sunk almost immediately, while the damaged submarine managed to escape and find refuge in Cape Town.

The communication systems had been seriously compromised and the submarine had suffered significant damage to its hull and engine. For the next 8 months, the crew worked tirelessly to find materials and repair the vessel.

During their stay in Cape Town, my grandfather and a small group of men were responsible for obtaining the necessary supplies not only for the submarine's repairs, but also for their everyday needs. After much hard work and resourcefulness, the submarine was deemed seaworthy, although it could only travel at the surface as the hull was still too fragile to withstand underwater pressure.

Eventually, they made their way back to their home port in France, unaware that the war had ended several months prior. Their communications equipment had been beyond salvageable.

One day, on a nice day (as my grandmother's sister would have said), my grandfather Marcel - who had been listed as MIA (missing in action) - returned to his hometown and became a local hero. No one from their small village had ever ventured so far and faced such adventures.

My grandfather became a well-known, admired, and respected figure in town. I knew him until I was about 7 years old, when he passed away.

Now, as an adult wandering the streets of Cape Town myself, I couldn't help but think that we would have had an amazing time if we had explored this city together.

After a lengthy chat with my mother, it was time to join the team for breakfast, which was the thing I was most looking forward to, besides taking a bath. It was a rare treat to have a meal that I didn't have to prepare myself. When I arrived at the hotel's lobby cafe, I saw Catherine, Luke, Katheryn, Carl, and Sven sitting at a large table, engaged in lively conversation.

"Good morning," I greeted them hoarsely before taking a seat and browsing the breakfast menu. My stomach grumbled as I tried to decide what to order; I was so hungry that I could have devoured the entire menu. I settled on Shakshuka Eggs, one of my favourite breakfast items to both make and eat.

> *Shakshuka eggs are cooked in a tomato-based sauce which is prepared using chopped red onion, garlic, diced red capsicum, a hint of chilli, cumin seeds, and a pinch of ground coriander and paprika. The eggs are then baked/poached in the sauce in the oven and topped with either feta or labneh and a sprinkling of fresh herbs (flat parsley, mint, coriander).*

The atmosphere was jovial and we all shared some laughs, recalling the chaotic situation we had found ourselves in when we arrived late the night before. It had been a relief to be back in Cape Town with more time on my hands, compared to the rushed 24 hours I had experienced before heading out to Antarctica. We chatted about the events of the season, and I thoroughly enjoyed my breakfast choice. After a couple of hours, the two K/Catherines headed back to the office for work. The rest of us turned our attentions to planning out our day. The weather was perfect – sunny, with a light breeze, and the temperature in the mid-20s.

As someone who was experiencing Cape Town for the first time, I was happy to go along with the rest of the gang. Carl suggested that we meet on his balcony at 11 a.m. and take an Uber to Hout Bay for lunch.

We all agreed to the plan and went back to our rooms to get ready, having arranged to meet again in an hour. Despite feeling a little groggy from the day before's events – a combination of a lack of sleep and too much alcohol - I decided to treat myself to another coffee on my balcony.

Standing on the balcony, I couldn't help but be taken aback by the exquisite view around me. To the right, the sun's rays danced upon the ocean's surface, creating a glittering spectacle that stretched as far as the eye could see. People strolled along the promenade, their silhouettes adding to the picturesque scene.

On the left, a series of idyllic bays unfurled like a hidden treasure waiting to be discovered, their crystal-clear waters flanked with a mesmerizing shade of turquoise that lapped gently against the shore, inviting visitors to explore their secrets.

In the distance, Lion's Head loomed over the city like a majestic guardian. Its towering rocky cliffs adorned with lush greenery at the base stood in stark contrast with the vibrant blue skies above. At 670 metres high, it was a sight to contemplate amidst the bustling city below. Its presence added to the natural beauty and allure of Cape Town, enhanced by its status as part of Table Mountain National Park. Above me, a group of six or seven tandem paragliders had launched from the gentle slopes of Signal Hill to the left of Lion's Head.

As I took in the stunning view, I was distracted by an increasingly foul smell in the air. I had noticed it earlier when I spoke with my mum, but now it was even stronger - a mixture of rotten eggs and rubbish!

At first, I attributed it to the nearby ocean or the city sewage, but something wasn't right! I walked around on the balcony, inspecting every corner and looking over the handrail, but I couldn't find the source. But as I returned to the table and sat down, the stench hit me hard. With a sinking feeling, I leaned closer to the duffle bag that I had left out overnight and realised the brutal truth - it was my clothes from Antarctica!

Despite my attempts to wash them while on the icy continent, they were now emitting a putrid odour, due to Cape Town's mid-20s temperature and 60% humidity being perfect for bacterial growth. I felt embarrassed and frustrated - what was I going to do with the clothes?

My initial solution option was to simply throw them away in a rubbish bin, but then I remembered that I might need them if I got the opportunity to return next season.

My thoughts were interrupted by a knock at the door, and I opened it to find a housekeeping lady standing there. Suddenly, an idea struck me. I asked her for a couple of large garbage bags, explaining that I would leaving in about ten minutes, and would then be out of my room for the rest of the day. In a hurry, I emptied my duffle bag onto the balcony and hastily repacked everything into a garbage bag, tightly knotting it shut. Just to be safe, I doubled up with another bag and sealed that as well. Since I didn't want any unpleasant smells from my dirty clothes lingering in my room during my stay in Cape Town, I decided to leave the duffle bag out on the balcony for the duration of my stay.

Feeling satisfied with my clever solution, I made my way down one floor to meet up with the rest of the crew. Carl's door was open, and Luke was already sitting outside on the balcony with him.

Carl had decided that our spirits needed lifting after the late arrival and festivities the day before, so he went to a nearby bottle shop and bought some shots of Kuemmerling, a semi-bitter German herb liquor. Eventually, we all gathered on the balcony, some looking worse than others, and Carl brought "the magic" beverage out of the mini bar fridge and each of us took a little bottle in hand and raised them in a toast to celebrate (once again!) the end of a fantastic season and the day ahead. May it be filled with fun and happiness! After a few drinks, our spirits had lifted, and we called for an Uber ride to take us to Chapmans Peak Hotel in Houts Bay.

Carl and Luke had been there before, and their reviews were excellent. We asked the driver to take us there by the scenic route so we could soak in the stunning views of Cape Town along the way. It was my first time seeing this side of the city and I was not disappointed. The road curved around hills and valleys until finally reaching Hout Bay, where the restaurant was nestled. Cape Town had really started to grow on me; I was already having such a good time and still had a few days ahead of me.

Upon arrival, we were greeted by friendly waiters and shown to a lovely table on the terrace overlooking the bay. It felt almost surreal to be sitting on a terrace overlooking the South Atlantic when less than 24 hours ago we had just arrived from Antarctica. As we sat down, the waiter asked if we would like any drinks before taking the food orders.

We all ended up ordering aperitifs, wines, beers, and all kinds of shots before even looking at food options. The whole day was filled with laughter and camaraderie among friends as we enjoyed our meals and continued to celebrate. It turned into a wild, carefree day with no plans or commitments whatsoever. We basked in the warm sun, surrounded by beautiful scenery, creating a treasured memory that would last for years.

As the day wore on, we left the restaurant; time seemed to slip away, and I lost any sense of where we were. We had decided to visit Patrick at his home, but after ringing the doorbell for some time, we realised he must not have been at home, or he was smart enough not to let a group of drunken fools in. So, we continued our pub crawl through the city.

From that point on, everything became hazy, and I can't recall any of our movements after leaving Patrick's house.

The next thing I knew, I was waking up on the ground in a Cape Town side street in the middle of the night. As I made my way towards the main street, I vaguely recognised the area and eventually, I found the way back to my hotel.

When I woke up the following morning, I was still fully dressed and lying on top of my bed. Feeling groggy and in need of refreshment, I took a quick shower before heading down to the cafe for breakfast.

My body craved something to boost my recovery, so I ordered a double espresso and a large freshly pressed orange juice to help recuperate from the previous day's boozy tour.

None of my friends were around and I considered going back to my room to rest after breakfast. However, just as that thought crossed my mind, my phone rang with Katheryn on the other end, her cheerful voice asking how I was doing.

"Hey there, Kath. I'm doing fine, how about you?" It was a lie, but I didn't want to bother her with my self-inflicted pain.

"Great. Listen, Patrick wants us all to meet up at a restaurant tonight. I've arranged for a shuttle bus to pick everyone up from the hotel at 5:30 pm. Could you let the others know? I've been trying to reach them, but no luck." I knew a perfectly good reason why she couldn't get through to anyone!

"Oh, and it's a fancy place, so if you guys have any nice casual clothes, that would be perfect," she added.

So now, I had two tasks on my hands:

Firstly, I needed a haircut and a shave badly, considering I looked like I'd been living in a cave for the past few months.

Secondly, I needed some decent clothes for that night, because my only remotely presentable items were buried somewhere in that smelly duffel bag out on the balcony, along with my Antarctic gear.

With those thoughts in mind, I headed towards the hotel exit in search of a hairdresser.

As I wandered down the main street and passed by a burger joint and cocktail bar, to my surprise, someone called out, *"Good morning, Seb! How are you today?"* But when I turned around, scanning the area for familiar faces, I couldn't see anyone I knew amongst the bustling crowd.

Then, all of a sudden, there was a man standing in front of me, tall and slender with an apron tied around his waist. He had a big smile on his face as he greeted me by name, but I couldn't place him. It didn't click until he mentioned our plans for that night, that he had been a waiter at the burger/cocktail joint, and we had been supposed to go back there for happy hour that day.

"Oh boy," I thought to myself. I had no memory of agreeing to anything, but I played along and told him our plans had changed, though we might make it tomorrow afternoon.

Then, I asked if he knew of any nearby hair salons or barbers.

"My aunt owns one just a few streets away," he said, drawing a simple map on a piece of paper and instructing me to tell her that he sent me. I thanked him and started walking in the direction he had pointed to.

I turned back one last time to ask his name, and he replied, - *"Andile!"* Well, that didn't ring any bells either. I must have been in a really bad state the day before if I couldn't even remember his name or the place!

But it didn't matter; I needed to get a haircut, a shave, and some clothes to go out for dinner later.

Several hours had passed, but in the end, my two missions proved successful. I had found Andile's aunt's hairdressing and barber salon (step one complete), and as I walked further down the street, I came upon a shop selling decent men's clothes.

As I made my way back to the hotel, I couldn't help but think about lunch. That's when I passed by an intriguing place - a large indoor food court with a bar in the centre, offering a view of the ocean. Without hesitation, I decided to take a quick walk-through.

The place was called The Mojo Market and even though it was just past midday, there was already an eclectic crowd gathered inside. The music playing throughout the place was pleasant, so I grabbed a pizza and a pint of Castle Lager - the local beer - and enjoyed my lunch while taking in the ocean view. While I was sitting there, Luke happened to pass by on his way to the office. He joined me for a quick sit-down, and we shared the pizza, which also served as his breakfast.

I asked him about what had happened after we left Patrick's house yesterday, but he couldn't remember much either. I then told him about how I had woken up in a side street before making my way back to the hotel. *"Seb, you can't sleep in the streets of Cape Town, it's not safe,"* he scolded with a laugh.

After Luke left for work, I continued towards the hotel and ran into Felix. I hadn't seen him since our arrival in Cape Town, but I noticed that he, too, had gotten a haircut - meaning he had to also be aware of the evening's dinner arrangements. I asked him what his plans were and he said that he was just trying to find a place for a light lunch and a drink, so I told him about the Mojo Market, and with a blink of an eye we were both on our way back there looking for some food for him. We ended up back at the pizza place and got hold of a high table to enjoy some premium ocean views for the next couple of hours, before returning to the hotel and getting ready to catch the shuttle bus that would take us to the restaurant for dinner.

The bus arrived right on cue to transport us to the venue in Constantia, which had been chosen by Patrick. Our office team, made up of Katheryn, Tarryn, Shaun, Catherine, and Gareth, had already gathered and were eagerly awaiting our arrival.

The place was surrounded by tall, leafy trees that created a natural canopy over the outdoor terrace where we waited for Patrick and Robyn to arrive while enjoying some pre-dinner drinks. The wooden tables and chairs were spread out under the trees, which were surrounded by bright, blooming flowers in various shades. The sunlight filtered through the leaves, creating a warm and inviting atmosphere. Birds could be seen flitting about, their songs filling the air with a gentle melody.

Beyond the terrace, the rest of the restaurant was a charming old building with large windows and a rustic feel. I sat down next to Katheryn, who had a serious expression on her face.

She turned towards me and immediately started talking. *"Seb,"* she asked, *"did you spend the night sleeping on the street?"* Her tone was full of concern.

I thought to myself how quickly news travelled as I glanced at Luke, who had been in the office earlier that day and knew about my escapade.

In an attempt to diffuse the situation, I replied, *"Well, not the whole night. I just took a quick nap to recover."* Katheryn's gaze was stern as she firmly said to me, *"Seb, it's not safe to sleep on the streets at night. You could have been killed!!"*

My response was quick, as I tried to diffuse the situation: *"No need to worry, Kath. If anyone had seen me, they would have assumed I was already dead!"*

The group laughed at my joke and it seemed to have done the trick as the conversation shifted to other topics. Once again, I had found a clever way out of a tricky situation.

The menu had a variety of options, from game meat to seafood and vegetarian dishes. We decided to order some appetisers to share while waiting for our mains. The biltong (dried cured meat) and droëwors (dried sausage) platters were an instant hit among the group. As we sipped on our drinks and nibbled on appetisers, Patrick stood up and began to speak. He wanted to express his gratitude towards every one of us for our hard work and dedication throughout a season that had led to the growth of White Desert.

From that moment on, I no longer saw Patrick and Robyn as my bosses, but rather, as friends and colleagues. We all worked together with a common passion and goal: to share our values with guests and fellow adventurers who joined us on our journeys to Antarctica.

Shortly after, our mains arrived - I had ordered the Bobotie, which was a traditional South African dish made of minced meat, egg custard, and topped with raisins and almonds. It was served with yellow rice, chutney, and sambal (a spicy condiment). The flavours were unlike anything I had ever tasted before - it was sweet, savoury, and had just the right amount of spice. As the dinner went on, we continued to chat and exchange stories from the past season. We talked about our experiences on ice as well as in the office, highlighting the strong bond that existed between us as a team.

Eventually, Patrick suggested moving to the bar for some dessert or cocktails, but I was in the mood for a digestif. When Felix asked if it was okay to have a cognac instead of a cocktail, I knew we were partners in crime. Without hesitation, I ordered two glasses of the finest cognac, which turned out to be one of the best we had ever tasted!

As the night came to an end, the shuttle bus took us back to the hotel. I couldn't help but feel grateful and lucky to have been a part of White Desert. If they asked for my services next season, I knew I would gladly join in on the adventure without any hesitation.

The next day, I woke up again bright and early as usual and headed down to the café, which had just opened.

As I sat down, I noticed that the usually fast and efficient service seemed a bit slower today. No one seemed to take notice of me until the waiter eventually brought me my double espresso, remembering that it was my usual order every other day. It's those little moments that differentiate good service from outstanding service.

With only a few days left, I was determined to make the most of my time in Cape Town.

There were two projects on my mind for the trip: visiting Robben Island and indulging in my hobby of rooftop bar exploration.

After finishing my breakfast, I called for an Uber ride to take me to V&A Waterfront, where tours departed hourly, for a 3.5-hour guided tour. Robben Island is a small island located in Table Bay, part of the City of Cape Town. It's renowned for being a world heritage site, and for being the place where Nelson Mandela was held prisoner during his incarceration in 1964 by South Africa's Apartheid regime.

The moment I stepped out of the boat, I could feel a wave of emotions seemingly coming from all directions. As we walked along the pathways, I couldn't help but marvel at how resilient the inmates must have been, and how much they had withstood throughout history. Everywhere I looked, there were stories from former prisoners that had served time there, and their accounts of pain and suffering still lingered in the air. But there was also hope; against all odds, some had survived and eventually prevailed over an oppressive regime that wanted to break their spirits. We visited some old prison cells, including Mandela's cell, which still stood as a reminder of past experiences and the ability to overcome any challenge ahead. We even got a chance to see some artefacts from his time here that included letters he wrote while imprisoned, as well as personal items he had used during his stay on the island. As we made our way back towards our boat, we stopped for one last look at the spectacular views around us before beginning our journey back to Cape Town. The day we had just shared left a lasting impact on everyone aboard – it was an unforgettable experience.

It was now midday, and I realised that I had the entire afternoon and evening to devote to my next project: rooftop bars. After a quick search on my phone, I found several options in the nearby Silo district, which was where my journey of discovery began.

My first stop was Red Rooftop Bar, which was located on top of the Radisson Hotel. Its stunning view comprised the Waterfront shipyard and the cityscape, with Table Mountain as its backdrop.

As I sat there taking in the scenery, I couldn't help but reflect on the story my mother had shared about my grandfather's time in Cape Town over seventy years before. At that moment, I felt a deeper connection to him than ever before - we both shared a special bond with this city. After some more indulgence at that beautiful venue, I pulled out my phone again to find my next destination and ordered an Uber ride. I spent the rest of my day hopping from one place to another until late in the evening.

On another occasion, my friend Louis, who worked as a mechanic for White Desert and lived around 50km east of Cape Town, offered to pick us up from our hotel and took us on a scenic drive through the beautiful wine region of Stellenbosch and Franschhoek before having a braai (barbecue) at his house.

That Sunday morning, Lukas, Jean-Seb, and I gathered in the hotel lobby and waited for Louis to pick us up and take us on a scenic drive through this magnificent, world-famous wine- making region.

The rolling hills and vibrant green vineyards were a sight to behold as we drove down the winding roads. Along the way, we stopped at various local tasting boutiques to try out the best wines and learn about the process behind each bottle. The pride and passion of those involved in winemaking were evident everywhere we went, and naturally, we couldn't resist buying a few bottles to indulge in later with lunch.

As we ventured deeper into the valley, we came upon charming villages with cobbled streets lined with quaint cafes, restaurants, and shops selling local delicacies and handmade goods from the region. After a brief stop to purchase some meat for lunch, we arrived at Louis's house, where he welcomed us with a traditional South African braai and showcased the renowned hospitality of the country.

We indulged in some delicious dishes, then went to enjoy the refreshing breeze on his veranda, chatting well into the afternoon before realising how quickly time had passed. I couldn't help but feel immensely grateful to have experienced such an amazing country first-hand. A few hours later, after Louis had dropped us off back in Cape Town, his car disappeared into the night and our hearts sank with it.

We ventured into the hotel bar, desperately craving one final taste of this amazing city before we were torn apart again. The clock struck 10:00 pm and we knew our time together had dwindled to mere hours.

As our exciting season drew to a close, the pressure mounted, and we began to get ready to go back to our ordinary lives on opposite sides of the world. But of course, there was also a rush of exhilaration as we prepared for our journeys home after months of incredible adventures.

Even home has its own allure, as I went to sleep for one last time, I felt its pull more keenly than I had for a while.

Markets and festivals

The flight home took me from Cape Town through Dubai and Singapore, and I arrived in Brisbane at 6.00 am. It was the best time to fly into Brisbane as the sun had just breached the horizon, the air was still light and crisp, and the view over the city was spectacular. It was always quiet at that time of day, which made all the immigration and customs clearances a breeze. In no time at all, I was out of the airport and waiting for the train for the final leg of my trip - heading home to the Gold Coast.

The next day, I wasted no time in getting back in touch with the market organisers to secure a location for my pretzel stall for the following week.

That first market would be an opportunity to catch up with friends, but most importantly, to re-adjust to life in a busy society and re-adjust to the hot, sunny, humid end of summer in Queensland.

The week went by in a blink of an eye and before I realised, it was Tuesday again, meaning I had to get ready for the market in Brisbane city. I woke up early on Wednesday morning, feeling a mix of excitement and nervousness coursing through my veins. It had been months since I had last set up my pretzel stall at the Brisbane city market, and I couldn't help but wonder if people would still remember me.

The Brisbane farmer's market was a tumultuous and intoxicating frenzy, brimming with bustling stalls overflowing with interesting, locally sourced produce. The strong scents of freshly baked delights and sizzling meats wafted through the air, mingling with the sweet scent of ripe fruits and the earthy aroma of vegetables. Amidst the chaos, people haggled and bartered with fervour, creating a palpable sense of community through supporting their beloved local businesses. Music echoed throughout the city square, adding to the lively atmosphere as shoppers weaved through crowds to peruse an endless variety of goods.

As I returned to Brisbane after my expedition in Antarctica, I was hit with the jarring contrast of being thrust back into the chaotic rhythm of city life, but it was a welcome assault on the senses. The vibrant energy and constant buzz of activity enveloped me once again, like a familiar embrace from an old friend. It felt like coming home after a long absence, and being engulfed in the pulsing beat of the city was nothing short of exhilarating.

The market also provided an opportunity to reconnect with old friends. Greg had a stall next to mine, where he sold hot smoked salmon and several other smoked items such as tofu, cashew nuts, and chicken. As I chatted with him, my hands moved quickly to set up my stall.

The familiar smell of warm dough wafted through the air as I was cooking the pretzels. Finally, with a satisfying ding, the timer went off and I eagerly opened the door to reveal the shiny golden-brown pretzels, adorned with flecks of salt. The aroma was irresistible, drawing hungry customers in from every direction. As they took their first bites, their eyes widened with delight at the combination of crispy exterior and soft, chewy centre. Freshly baked pretzels are truly a mouthwatering experience that I still believe can't be matched by any other treat at the market, and with each batch that came out of the oven, I felt a renewed sense of purpose.

As the morning went on, more of my regular customers trickled in, delighted at the sight of my stall being back. The day went by in a flash, and I was happy to return home as it had taken its toll on me, mainly due to the hot and heavy weather conditions, but also because I was still battling jet lag.

On Thursday, I woke up early despite the busy and tiring day at the market, and I made the best use of the time by planning for the year ahead. I had overheard a conversation between two fellow stallholders who were not only doing markets but also attending festivals and events on the Gold Coast and Brisbane.

I went online and in no time, I had identified several events throughout the year that would be suitable for my product.

I selected four that I was keen to attend:

The annual *Blues on Broadbeach music festival*, held in mid-May, which would draw a large crowd to the beautiful beaches of the Gold Coast with its lineup of both international and Australian blues musicians. The lively streets, venues, and parks of Broadbeach would come alive with performances during this popular event.

The ***Cooly Rocks on Festival*** takes place in Coolangatta on the Gold Coast, typically in early June. This was a one-of-a-kind event that combined music and car shows with numerous classic car displays, retro fashion showcases, live performances, dance parties, and parades. It was a highly anticipated and beloved festival for its attendees.

The annual ***French Festival*** in **Brisbane**, held near the celebration of French National Day on July 14th, was a well-known display of French culture, featuring music, cuisine, and lifestyle.

The ***Gold Coast Show*** took place over three days in August, bringing together agriculture and modern culture through competitions, demonstrations, free entertainment, thrilling rides, and a spectacular fireworks display.

My schedule was carefully arranged so that I could still attend my usual markets without too much interruption, other than a few weekend absences.

On top of that, I had just received an email from my cousin Claire in France, informing me of her desire to visit Australia for a holiday and help out at the markets. The timing couldn't have been better! It would also be a great opportunity for us to spend time together and get to know each other better. Due to our significant age gap and my frequent travelling, we hadn't spent much time together in the past.

With my events planned out, I immediately began brainstorming new flavours of pretzels to experiment with. My goal was to create even more unique and funky combinations.

To make this happen, I reached out to my friend Stephan, a German butcher who had previously provided me with bacon and other deli meats during my time at Sea World Resort.

I inquired if he could create some mini cheese kransky sausages to my exact specifications. Once wrapped in pretzel dough, they resembled a cross between a sausage roll and a hot dog. The mini sausages provided by Stephan were a game-changer!

With every bite of the succulent smoked cheese Kransky pretzels, an explosion of flavours would flood your taste buds with notes of paprika, mustard seeds, black pepper, and a subtle touch of garlic.

To add even more taste, I sprinkled them with smoked salt that I made myself in the nearby Tallebudgera Valley. The result was simply UNBELIEVABLE!

As soon as I had set up my stall and displayed the new pretzels, I could see people's eyes light up with interest. Some of my regular clients came over, eager to try out the new creation, while others stopped by after smelling the enticing scent spreading through the market.

I offered samples to anyone passing by and watched the delight appear on their faces after taking a bite. I even had some customers coming back for seconds and thirds!

The feedback from Joe, his team at the market and my regular clients was overwhelmingly positive. *"I've never tasted anything like this before!"* one customer had exclaimed, while another said, *"These are simply incredible!"*

I couldn't believe how successful they had proven on the first day. As I continued selling throughout the morning, word of mouth spread quickly. People started coming up to ask specifically for "the smoked cheese kransky ones" rather than just regular pretzels. By 11am, I had completely sold out of all my stock and was left with a long list of pre-orders for the next market. I was very satisfied, and I thought that perhaps I should have a "special flavour" every so often, to breathe new life into the regular selection and keep my loyal customers intrigued.

On Sunday morning, as I was at the Arts and Craft market, Stephan and his family walked through the market and stopped at my stall. I was busy and didn't have much time for him, so instead I treated him with one of the Kransky pretzels and told him that I would call him and arrange to catch up together later in the week.

Not even a few minutes had passed when I could see him coming back. But this time, it was no casual market cruising - he was darting straight for my stall. My first thought was that he didn't like the idea of mixing a sausage and a pretzel since his ethnic background was from Germany.

I braced myself for a culinary red card, but it turned out to be the complete opposite. He bought another 6 of them and told me that he loved them, in his broken but perfectly understandable English.

I realised that what I had was the perfect product for marketgoers: an easy, satisfying snack that could be eaten at any time of day. My fellow expedition members would have loved this, I thought to myself. It had been quite a journey, starting from making soft pretzels for a beer-tasting event in Antarctica to becoming a successful entrepreneur, selling my creations at local farmer's markets.

It had taken hard work, patience, dedication, and creativity to reach this point, but I had now earned myself a reputation and a fast-spreading nickname as "The Pretzel God."

As my business continued to grow, I decided to offer catering services for special events. I started with small private parties, weddings, and family gatherings, but soon enough, larger events started to come in by word of mouth. People were eager to try something new at their next gathering, and I was more than happy to oblige.

May arrived promptly and so did my cousin, Claire. I quickly found that it was nice to have her around and I enjoyed getting to know her better. Despite our limited acquaintance, I found that we shared many similar qualities that also reminded me of my mother in her youth. As a result, we got along famously, bonding over our quick wit, sense of humour, and can-do attitude. Claire's plans were simple: rent a camper van and explore as much of Australia as possible, and in between, she wanted to be a part of the markets - but mostly the big events.

Having her around was a bonus once she became comfortable with the van. I vividly recall the day when I entrusted her with the keys to the van and asked her to drive us around for the day.

It was an exhilarating experience that I will never forget. Not only had she never driven outside of the EU before, but she also had to adjust to driving a manual vehicle and changing gears with her left hand (as we drive on the left in Australia). To make things easier, I reminded her that the driver should always be close to the centre of the road if she ever felt unsure of her positioning.

With those final words of advice, we set off across the city. Overall, the day went relatively smoothly, and by late afternoon, Claire seemed confident in her driving abilities.

But just as those thoughts had crossed my mind, she had made a daring turn at a traffic light and cut right across oncoming traffic, which prompted my heart to race with fear and anticipation.

It was too late to say anything or even for a short prayer, as we were already engaged in the intersection!

Instead, I closed my eyes and held my breath, hoping for some kind of divine intervention to guide us safely through.

Miraculously, we did make it through unharmed, as if a guardian angel had been looking down on us at that precise moment. We both let out a relieved laugh, sharing the same casual attitude toward the near accident. After a brief discussion about what had gone wrong, we continued with our journey.

From then on, I knew I could trust Claire's driving skills - she had proven herself to be competent and reliable behind the wheel. But it also made me realise that I should stick to my current job and never consider becoming a driving instructor!

Having Claire by my side during market days was a great help, but her presence during big events was invaluable. I remembered the hustle and bustle of preparations for the French festival in particular. I had even rebranded the stall as "Saveurs d'Alsace" by The Pretzel Nook to represent our home region in France. It was a rare opportunity to share a piece of our culture with those on the opposite side of the globe. During the planning process, I came up with another brilliant idea: selling woodfired chestnuts, just like the ones from my childhood.

Unfortunately, all the suppliers on the Gold Coast told me it was too late in the season for chestnuts. But luck was on my side once more, as Claire happened to be interstate in Adelaide (South Australia) at the same time and was able to source some extra-large chestnuts and bring back 120 kg just in time for the French Festival. The event was a huge success, drawing crowds from all over South East Queensland who wanted to immerse themselves in French culture.

The atmosphere was lively, filled with music and dance performances. Our stall was conveniently located next to our friends Pierre and Stephanie's stall, Le Fromage Yard. We had planned it that way so that we could help each other out if needed or get a bit of moral support during the long days. And boy were they long!

Our days began early in the morning, as we prepared our delectable pretzels and set up the stall. Our selection was straightforward, with a traditional salted option, two savoury and two sweet pretzels.

Once they were baked, we would add grated cheddar and a touch of our garlic butter made with French demi-sel butter, fresh thyme, rosemary, chives, and garlic. These were then placed back in the oven, which would intensify the buttery garlic scent and melt the cheddar into a light gratiné topping.

For the second savoury option, we took baked pretzels and topped them with grated Tomme cheese, tangy chunks of Roquefort, and crunchy walnut pieces. As they heated up, the cheeses and walnuts melted together in a deliciously gooey mixture. Each bite burst with a combination of rich, nutty flavours and velvety textures. Our inspiration for the sweet pretzels came from traditional almond croissants. To achieve a crispy top on these pretzels, we sprinkled raw sugar on them at the start of cooking which caramelised and set after baking, giving a slightly toffee-like finish.

We also created a frangipane using ground almonds, sugar, eggs, and butter (of course!) which we added on top of the cooked pretzels along with chocolate buttons, before returning them to the oven for a few minutes to allow everything to melt and bind together.

Our second indulgent option quickly became a fan favourite, rivalled only by the traditional salted pretzels. As soon as they came out of the oven, they were coated in a dusting of cinnamon sugar that had been expertly combined with orange zest for an explosion of taste in every bite. This simple yet incredibly flavourful combination kept customers coming back for more. Claire and I tirelessly worked throughout the day, serving customers, making sales, and having fun along the way. One of the most cherished and highly anticipated moments of the festival was the lively French Cancan performance that graced the main stage multiple times a day.

The vibrant dancers moved with infectious energy, kicking and twirling to the lively beat of the music in their colourful ruffled skirts and feathered headpieces. Their exuberant movements and bold expressions captured the attention of every onlooker, drawing them into a world of excitement and joy. The air was filled with the sounds of clapping and cheering, creating a jubilant atmosphere that lingered long after the performance had ended. It was a display of pure talent and passion, leaving an unforgettable impression on all who were fortunate enough to witness it. Like a magnetic force, it never failed to draw in a crowd. Our eyes would often stray from our stall, lured in by the mesmerising spectacle before us. It was impossible not to be captivated by the dazzling display of colours and energy that seemed to radiate from every dancer. We were like curious children, peeking through the cracks just to catch another glimpse of the magic happening before our very eyes.

On Sunday afternoon, we were both caught up serving customers when suddenly, we heard loud cheers and applause coming from the main stage. We knew it was time for the final performance of the day – a grand finale featuring all of the festival's performers.

It was moments like these that made all of our hard work worth it. We were exhausted but also overjoyed to be a part of such a spectacular event. As the sun set on Sunday night and the festival came to a close, we packed up our stall, completely drained, but also feeling immensely fulfilled.

Our products, including the extra-large chestnuts Claire had brought from Adelaide, were all sold out and we couldn't have been happier with how the weekend had gone.

Dealing with unpredictable weather was one of the biggest challenges for market stallholders. Even though we loved spending our weekends outdoors and interacting with customers, Mother Nature didn't always cooperate.

Trading at markets in the rain took determination and resilience, as it could be a long and difficult day. I remember one specific Sunday, when Claire and I woke up to the sound of heavy rain on the rooftop at home. Our first instinct was to check the weather forecast, hoping for signs of improvement by the time we had to set up our stall.

Unfortunately, the forecast predicted continuous rain throughout the day. We groaned together, knowing it would be a tough day ahead.

But we reminded ourselves that we were committed to our business and loyal customers, who would be there come rain or shine.

As we drove through the rain to the market site, we could see puddles forming on the road and dark clouds looming overhead. By the time we had unloaded the equipment from the van at our designated stall spot, both of us were already drenched. We took a collective deep breath and began setting up our stall, doing our best to protect our equipment from getting wet, although everything seemed to absorb moisture from the air.

Despite the difficult conditions, we were surprised to see that there had been quite a few customers at the market. Some had come equipped with umbrellas and raincoats, while others just embraced the wet weather and strolled around with a smile on their face.

We quickly realised that those brave customers were our key to success on that rainy day. However, as the day went on, the rain continued to pour heavily, making it increasingly challenging to keep everything dry. We kept a close eye on our products, constantly wiping away any water droplets that threatened to ruin the pretzels. It was a constant battle against the elements. At one point, we even thought that we would have to shut down as the strong winds threatened to knock over our display shelves.

But through all of that chaos, something unexpected happened – the stallholders all bonded with each other through adversity. Giggles and jokes were exchanged between us all, making the day more bearable. In moments when we felt overwhelmed and discouraged, it was their support and encouragement that kept us going. As the market came to an end and we started packing up our soggy belongings, Claire turned to me with a tired but satisfied smile on her face and said, *"Today may have been tough, but I feel like we conquered it!"*

I couldn't have agreed more. The rain may have put a damper on our spirits and the stalls, but it also highlighted our resilience and determination as market vendors. Days like this served as a reminder of why I had embarked on this venture - not just for my love of food and community, but also for the gratification of overcoming obstacles and adversity!

As early August approached, I received an email from Katheryn, asking if I was still planning to return for another season in Antarctica. For me, the decision was a no-brainer.

My entire year revolved around the markets and events leading up to my summer in Antarctica, so I couldn't wait for November to arrive. It wasn't work that brought me back year after year; I also relished the opportunity to change my surroundings and tackle a different role, all while reconnecting with my friends at White Desert. I eagerly replied, confirming my return and expressing my excitement to be back on ice.

As soon as I hit send, a wave of nostalgia washed over me as I reminisced about my previous seasons. I had missed the endless, satisfying hours spent toiling in the kitchen, meticulously crafting dishes for our eager staff members and appreciative guests. The awe-inspiring scenery surrounding our camp provided a constant source of inspiration and wonder. Then, there was the bond formed with the dedicated team members, which was like that of a family united in our love for the frozen continent, and in sharing that passion with others. It was more than just a job - it was a fulfilling, enriching lifestyle that I had been longing for, and I knew I wouldn't trade it for anything in the world or pass up on an opportunity to return.

As August progressed, I could feel the anticipation building up inside of me. Soon, it would be time for my last big event of the season - The Gold Coast show.

The preparation for this event was intense and required weeks of planning. We ordered ingredients and supplies, brainstormed new pretzel options, and organised our set-up for optimal efficiency. The day before the event, we arrived at the showgrounds to set up amidst the bustle of other vendors and performers rehearsing their acts.

Without delay, we got to work on our stall until it was ready for business. Taking a moment to appreciate our hard work, we looked around with satisfaction as everything was set up and ready for the onslaught. The four-day show was a whirlwind of activity, promising to be full-on from start to finish.

From early morning until late at night, we constantly cooked pretzels, served customers, and cleaned up after each rush. It wasn't just about setting up our stalls and cooking, though; it was also about immersing ourselves in the lively atmosphere of music, entertainment, carnivals, rides, and various events happening throughout the precinct.

Despite the chaos surrounding us, there were moments of pure happiness and contentment. As we worked as a cohesive team, sharing jokes and singing to the music in the background, I couldn't help but feel grateful for this experience - especially since it was Claire's final event. In just a few weeks, she would be returning to France after her time in Australia.

Amid the busy crowd, I caught sight of a familiar face - it was an old friend called Conrad. We had met almost thirty years before while he was backpacking through Europe. At the time, we were both working at a restaurant in Rüdesheim (Germany), and we even shared an apartment above the venue. After losing touch for a few years, he was now right there in front of the stall at the showground, performing the Lion dance with his Kung Fu team as a part of the event. We promised to catch up over a beer the following weekend, but for now, we were both busy with our respective responsibilities.

Claire and I were exhausted, but the sight of happy customers enjoying our pretzels and the show made it all worthwhile. Plus, we had met new people along the way. As mid-September approached, Claire's time in Australia was coming to an end and she would soon be returning to France.

As I drove her to the airport, we reminisced about the previous few months and shared some laughs together. It was really a coping mechanism to cover our sadness at parting ways, much like when I used to witness tourists leaving Greece in a previous job many years ago. Seeing them cry, not out of sadness, but out of having had a wonderful experience always brought me joy, and this time was no different.

With tears streaming down our cheeks, we bid our final farewells, knowing that it may be a while before we saw each other again. Emotions were heavy in the air and unspoken moments weighed heavily on our hearts. We held each other tightly, desperately trying to cling to the precious time spent together that would forever remain etched in our memories, as time slipped away like sand in an hourglass.

Parting ways was difficult, but the memories we created together would always stay with us.

WFR

2nd November 2019, Cape Town, South Africa

The airport was unusually quiet that morning, and I was grateful for the lack of crowds. It was nine o'clock, and all I wanted to do was check into my hotel, have a quick shower, then go and find my friends in Sea Point at the Mojo markets. It wouldn't be too hard a task, as it was where we usually gathered.

Today had been a breeze at the airport, with no one in line at customs clearance or immigration. Within minutes of gathering my bags, I was heading out of the big door leading to the airport exit. Amidst the limo drivers holding signs with names on them, I spotted mine and headed their way.

The driver gave me a nod and a big smile while continuing to speak into his cell phone, small earbuds lodged firmly in his ears. He grabbed my luggage, and we strode towards his automobile. Once I was in the back of the vehicle, I asked him if he was aware that I had to be dropped off at the President Hotel in Sea Point, and he nodded confidently.

White Desert had been using that private company for many years as it was the safest form of transportation. Though the driver's behaviour seemed odd, it didn't worry me more than that. All I wanted at the moment was to get to the hotel quickly; I wasn't in the mood for chit-chat anyway.

The driver started the engine and drove us on the freeway towards Cape Town CBD, still speaking on the phone in a language I couldn't understand. I watched the familiar streets of Cape Town's CBD pass by.

The usually bustling streets were strangely quiet; no people walking along the promenade, no traffic or buses honking, no passengers shouting desperately in search of commuters. It felt like all activity had been suspended - frozen in time.

It wasn't long before we arrived at the hotel, where I discovered what had been going on. Down by the outdoor swimming pool was an enormous screen and people were gathered around it cheering, laughing, singing, and drinking beers despite it being only 11 am. Of course, it was no ordinary day - it was the Rugby World Cup final and South Africa was taking on England! It goes without saying that rugby in South Africa is almost a way of life, part of the DNA.

So, I quickly put my bags down in my room and forwent my shower to get over to Mojo market and watch the match.

The air was thick with excitement and tension, and every bar and restaurant was overflowing with supporters wearing green and gold jerseys and waving flags. They had even dusted off the vuvuzelas from the football World Cup from a few years ago, and the noise of plastic horns filled the air.

You could feel the energy crackling in the atmosphere, delivering an electricity that promised something special. This was no mere rugby match; this was a battle for national pride. I knew right there and then that this would be a once-in-a- lifetime experience - one that would stay with me forever.

I made my way to the heart of the Mojo market, where a large screen had been set up for the game. Hundreds of people were inside, the atmosphere was intense, and I squeezed between the jostling bodies to get a better view.

It was just time for kick-off, and everyone fell to a hush in anticipation. When the referee finally blew his whistle, the crowd erupted into cheers.

It had begun - South Africa versus England, an epic battle for the ages! The energy grew as both teams pushed ahead with each attack, weaving a wild dance of movement around the field. As soon as the South African team scored, jubilant cheers and whoops flew through the air. Fans waved their flags and leapt up and down in frenzied adoration. The booming chorus of joy reverberated through the stadium, shaking its foundations with their immense power. There was a deep admiration for the national team - it was a real salute to South

African courage, and I immediately felt a part of it. With every second that passed, we sensed that victory could be ours.

As time wore on, the tension heightened until finally, it happened: when the referee blew his whistle one last time to announce that South Africa had triumphed!

The screams and shouting were so loud that they could have been detected on a seismograph, like an active volcano erupting. It was a memorable moment - one filled with laughter, joyful tears, and hugs as strangers embraced each other like long-lost friends. Faces lit up with excitement knowing that they'd been part of making history that day, the day that South Africa won their third Rugby World Cup title.

The next morning, after a raucous night of revelry that made me feel as if I were truly from South Africa, I trudged to the office to mingle with some colleagues and have a chat with Katheryn. As I stepped into the office, a wave of excitement washed over me in anticipation of the upcoming months at Wolf's Fang Runway (WFR). The camp had undergone some major upgrades and there would be more staff and guests to entertain. This meant more responsibility for me as I had to balance catering for both groups and ensure everything ran smoothly. Time management and organisational skills were crucial in the limited space of a tent with minimal facilities and resources. But there was also a sense of relief in knowing that the team would be able to assist with tasks like making water, which had previously been backbreaking and time-consuming for me.

Katheryn proudly gave me a glimpse of the new WFR plans. The guest tents had been transformed into luxurious havens, with plush bedding and modern amenities that rivalled any five-star hotel.

The once-plain dining area had also been elevated into a cosy space, with soft grey felt covering the walls and ceilings to insulate against the chilly weather outside. And what a view the guests would be treated to as they dined - the breathtaking Ulvetanna Peak looming majestically in the near distance, reaching towards the endless sky. It was truly an idyllic setting for a meal fit for royalty, surrounded by the pristine beauty of nature.

As we sipped our coffee in the office and continued discussing plans for the upcoming season, Katheryn shared with us that for that year, we would be anticipating a larger number of clients than ever before. Our reputation for providing unparalleled experiences and exceptional service had attracted the masses.

The first group to arrive was a family of 12 who had pre-booked their stay at WFR during the previous season. It was a proud moment for me, seeing how far we had come from Patrick's idea to becoming one of the most sought-after luxury camps in Antarctica. My mind was buzzing with ideas for how to elevate our clients' experiences even further that year. I was confident that with the support of my team and the fantastic upgrades at WFR, we could take things to new heights. I eagerly anticipated the challenges and opportunities that lay ahead.

We received confirmation of the weather forecast, and the conditions in Antarctica sounded perfect for that time of the year. Time was of the essence, and this meant we could fly over the vast expanse of the Southern Ocean as soon as possible and get to work.

Just like the year before, our layover in the city was brief. We wouldn't have any extra time to explore Cape Town until after the season ended, but that didn't bother me. I already had plans for when I returned.

As we approached WFR twenty-four hours later, my exhilaration grew, knowing that some familiar faces from previous seasons were eagerly awaiting my arrival on ice. I imagined them anticipating my arrival like hungry, caged lions waiting for their next meal.

The ice beneath us was smooth and flawless like glass, allowing our landing gear to glide effortlessly onto the frozen runway. It was as if nature itself wanted to create the perfect conditions for our plane to land safely. Moments of perfection like this were rare in this remote and unforgiving environment. Yet, at that time, I couldn't help but feel a sense of belonging and familiarity wash over me - it was almost as if I had finally returned home. Stepping off the plane,

I caught sight of Jean Seb and Felix working hard in the distance to ensure a quick turnaround for our flight. This was crucial to avoid any unexpected weather changes that could cause potential issues for the jet's departure. As an experienced chef, I fully recognised the value of organization when it came to achieving success in the kitchen.

Disorder and disarray only caused more problems and delays, something I refused to tolerate. I lived by the famous words of Benjamin Franklin:

"By failing to prepare, you are preparing to fail."

Years of practice taught me that anticipating the needs of my clients was crucial for an efficient operation and successful outcome. Neglecting preparation often led to disaster, which is why I arrived at WFR with every detail meticulously planned out.

As soon as we landed, my mind shifted into work mode. With laser focus and determination, I made my way swiftly to the familiar kitchen tent. The intense rays of the sun streamed through the small side windows; their brightness amplified by the glistening ice outside.

The light danced and reflected off every surface and tool in the room, creating a mesmerising display. The stainless-steel pots and pans shone from their racks, their handles glinting in the sun. My trained eyes swept over every inch of the space, double-checking that everything was in its proper place. In such a compact and fast-paced environment, even the slightest mistake could have catastrophic consequences for my dishes. After ensuring that every detail was perfect, I took a deep breath and let out a contented sigh.

With limited resources at hand as usual, I had to get creative with the menu planning and use ingredients sparingly. But this challenge excited me - it pushed me to come up with new and innovative dishes that surprised and delighted the staff.

As I prepped for dinner service, my thoughts drifted back to the challenges of the previous year, when we were still figuring out how to make things work in such an extreme environment. We faced setbacks like frozen equipment and unexpected snowstorms, but we persevered. Each obstacle only made us more determined to succeed. And now, here we were, ready to take on a new season with even more confidence and experience under our belts. Glancing at my watch, I saw that it was almost time for dinner.

With everything in order, I decided to take a quick walk around camp before the staff arrived. The sun was beginning its gradual descent behind Ulvetanna Peak, casting a warm golden light over the endless ice and snow. It was a magnificent light show that would soon disappear, with twenty-four-hour daylight on the way. I inhaled a deep breath of fresh Antarctic air, grateful to be back in this wonderful place once again.

As I made my way back to the kitchen tent, my excitement for the upcoming season's adventures and challenges grew stronger. We all gathered around the large makeshift dinner table, eagerly anticipating the meal I had prepared. Like the year before, I had decided on a quick and easy dish that required minimal ingredients; a Napolitana pasta that filled the room with its rich aroma, and for dessert, a chocolate pudding that would satisfy those with a sweet tooth.

The atmosphere was filled with warmth and joviality as we caught up on each other's lives since last season. At that moment, surrounded by such incredible people and sharing a simple, yet satisfying meal in the middle of nowhere, I knew I had found my soulmates. Among the familiar faces was one newcomer - a young lady from Wales named Elinor, who would be our resident Doctor for the first part of the season before another lady, Doctor Tash from Scotland, would take over from her around the end of December.

Being a doctor in Antarctica could be challenging - not because of the workload, but because of its scarcity. Thankfully, medical crises were infrequent, which allowed the doctor to assist with other duties at the camp during their spare time. From my observation, those with a few hours free seemed to gravitate towards the kitchen, including medical staff. It was a cosy and inviting atmosphere that was always warm and usually involved the comforting scent of coffee. There was also an abundance of snacks for people to nibble on as they mingled.

As the evening wore on, we all sat at the big dining table, some of us playing cards while others caught up with friends. A few people sat quietly reading a book. It was such a simplistic way of life and I had been longing to come back to it, with limited connection to the outside world, news, social media, or current affairs.

The next morning marked the beginning of a busy and exciting season. I had spent the previous day sorting through the kitchen, but the limited space and frequent deliveries for the clients made it a constant challenge to keep everything in order.

Another important task was to tackle the chaotic guest dining area and lounge, which resembled a chaotic disaster zone, with furniture scattered everywhere. Boxes and containers were strewn about the place, filled to the brim with various items such as dishes and toiletries. It looked as though a tornado had swept through, leaving behind a mess that seemed impossible to organize. With an overwhelming number of items to arrange, including glassware, rugs, cushions, and blankets, I couldn't help but wonder how we would find a place for everything.

Fortunately, Lily was there to lend her assistance, ensuring that our clients' needs were taken care of with utmost attention. Together, Lily and Elie (Dr Elinor) had devoted themselves to setting up the guest area of the tent for the arrival of our first group the following week. As we unpacked and arranged, the atmosphere inside the tent was energetic and vibrant, accompanied by background music to spur us on as we rearranged furniture and hung decorations.

Outside, the sky was still a brilliant blue and the sun provided warm rays to keep us full of vigour. With both the doors and windows open, we were able to fully appreciate the beautiful day. In the distance, Jean Seb and Felix meticulously drove the PistenBully vehicles to groom the ice runway in preparation for the next plane. It wasn't just a perfect day for organising and preparing for the guests, though - it was also ideal for starting another big project: building an outdoor bar made from stunning blue ice.

Andrei and Dimitri were tasked with this challenging job before they headed over to set up and maintain Dixie's camp. After a few days of hard work, both projects had been completed and we were left with a stunning outdoor ice bar.

On stepping into the tent, one would hardly have recognised the chaotic maze that it had been just days earlier. The transformation was remarkable; warm and inviting, with a touch of sophistication.

On the west side, a small porch greeted guests, offering a spot for them to shed their jackets, gloves, and beanies. In the main area, the spacious open layout revealed itself in all its glory.

A chic bar blended seamlessly into a modern dining area comprising a beautiful large wooden table and several lavish, fur-covered chairs.

The atmosphere of luxury and comfort continued into an exquisite lounge area, featuring a large leather sofa adorned with plush pillows and fur accents. In the centre of the lounge stood a large, industrial-looking coffee table atop a magnificent rug and in the corner, adding both warmth and elegance to the space, an elegant gas stove was already lit, with several steel racks hanging on the wall nearby, filled with Antarctic literature and other books about famous explorers.

When WFR was first set up, our equipment was scarce and basic. Reflecting on it, I realised it was a blessing in disguise. There was very little storage available, and organizing supplies was a challenging task, with only a few essential pots, pans, and trays at my disposal. I had to work smartly and effectively, with every ingredient being used to its fullest potential. The advantage of this, of course, was having fewer dishes to wash! With no access to running water, we expended tremendous effort digging and melting ice for fresh water, but it made us all aware of our water consumption, which dropped to an average of 10-20 litres per person per day.

The next day would mark the arrival of our first group of clients, and everything was perfectly in place. The camp was fully equipped with amenities, including hot showers and clean toilets – this might not seem like much, but in the harsh realm of Antarctica, this was true luxury. I made myself busy planning meals for both clients and staff for the upcoming week, thoughtfully considering each individual's dietary needs and preferences.

Cooking with limited resources had become an enjoyable challenge that I embraced wholeheartedly. Life off-grid really reminded us all of the simple pleasures in life and the value of resourcefulness. We were all united by our love for adventure and determination to make the best out of any situation that came our way. Of course, our meticulously crafted plans were once again thrown off course by the ever-changing weather.

The serene, sunny days we had been enjoying gave way to a sudden forecast of possible high winds, just in time for the arrival of the jet. With this new information in mind, Lily, Elie, and I scrambled to come up with a contingency plan for the morning of the expected arrival. Overnight, the wind had picked up and though it wasn't too strong, it would still make any outdoor welcome drinks uncomfortable - especially for guests who were not yet accustomed to the freezing temperatures. We quickly sprang into action, setting up a bar inside the guest lounge within the tent as an alternative should the wind persist.

We knew all too well that in Antarctica, even on clear, sunny days, the wind chill factor could make it feel much colder. Imagine a bone-chilling day of -17°, with added gusts of wind travelling at a gentle 15km/h. The biting cold air would whip against your face and seep through every layer of clothing, making it feel more like an icy -25°.

But if the wind suddenly ceased its relentless howling and all was still, it would really only feel like a bearable -4°. This is why monitoring wind speed was crucial for us; it could dramatically alter our perception of temperature at any given moment. It was quite a fickle companion - sometimes gentle and calming, other times raging with a ferocity that threatened to sweep us off our feet.

On one particular day, the phrase "frozen to the bone" finally made perfect sense to me. The sub-zero temperatures relentlessly penetrated the confines of my tent throughout the night. My polar sleeping bag was meant to withstand the conditions, but even with multiple layers of clothing, a beanie, woollen gloves, and thick socks, I still felt the intense coldness right inside my bones. Desperate for warmth, I stumbled into the kitchen tent and stood in front of the gas heater, the heat radiating onto my frozen body. I stayed there until my pants began to smoke from the proximity, but even then, I couldn't seem to shake off the relentless chill that had overcome my body. That day was without a doubt the coldest and most uncomfortable experience of my life thus far.

With only thirty minutes until landing, the wind suddenly shifted direction but still felt too forceful for our liking. Using our two-way radio system, I contacted Luke in the "comms box" to check on the current wind speed. He confirmed that it had indeed changed direction and dropped back down to 15km/h, prompting a collective sigh of relief. Elie had been assigned the task of greeting the guests upon their arrival. She had already positioned herself near the disembarking point when she overheard a conversation and interjected: *"Seb, the wind isn't too strong right now, I think we can have the welcome drinks outside at the ice bar."*

Lily and I exchanged unsure glances, feeling that it might still be too windy. As we scanned the horizon, we spotted a small dot moving closer and realized that it was the jet carrying our guests. We knew we had to make a quick decision as it would only be a matter of minutes before it landed. I noticed that the wind seemed to be dying down, so I turned to Lily and said, instinctively, *"Let's grab everything we've prepared inside and take it to the ice bar now."*

We hurried towards the tent together, rushing back and forth between the lounge and ice bar with –an array of glasses, drinks, and canapés. In true Antarctic fashion, it all came down to a matter of seconds as Elie led the group of 12 guests towards us at the ice bar.

They walked at various intervals, some eager to meet us while others were captivated by the breathtaking landscape and taking every opportunity to snap photos. Lily gracefully walked towards the group, her bright smile lighting up her face as she extended a welcoming hand and said, *"Welcome to the icy wonderland of Antarctica. I'm Lily, your host for the week."*

Her voice was warm and welcoming, and I did my best to follow her lead as I stepped forward with confidence, *"And I'm Seb, your chef for the duration of your stay."* The sense of relief on their faces was palpable as we reassured them that they would be well-cared for and would not go hungry during their stay. It was a small gesture, but it made all the difference in easing any worries they may have had about their trip.

Elie, Lily, and I served champagne and welcome cocktails to the guests behind the bar while Luke, the camp manager, introduced himself. The three French mountain guides also arrived, making our welcoming party complete.

We couldn't believe our luck - the wind had died down, the sun was shining, there were only a few clouds in the sky, and the temperature was perfect. It was great to meet the guests, and I had a good feeling about the upcoming week.

I bonded with Raj in particular. He was the patriarch of the family and their main point of contact, so it made sense to ask him about meal preferences and requirements. He assured me that they were all easy to please and just wanted simple, tasty, nutritious meals to share as a family. I promised to take care of them and told them to let me know if they had any special requests. Raj then returned to his family to discuss activities for the next few hours before dinner. Meanwhile, I checked the menu for the week and went through the food supplies that had been delivered by the jet earlier.

The idea was refreshingly straightforward: Instead of serving individual plates, I would prepare the planned meals for the week and serve them as sharing platters. It was a welcome change and surprisingly easier for me to manage. And I didn't stop there - for certain dishes, I went above and beyond by personally serving them to the guests at the table. Each dish was carefully arranged on beautiful platters, like a work of art waiting to be devoured. The chatter at the dining table and the laughter of my satisfied guests filled the room, creating a warm and joyous atmosphere. Not only it was more interactive, but also it allowed me to speak with everyone and find out more about what kind of dishes would make them happy over the week.

It may have been our first group of guests, but the team's hard work had paid off as we were well-prepared, and everything was running like clockwork. As the evening went on, the clients migrated to the lounge where they unwound around the cosy gas fire.

My day was almost over, but before I could rest, I needed to inform the group about breakfast arrangements for the next day. Raj asked me what time he could come by in the morning for a cup of tea or a coffee; being an early riser, he usually woke up at 5:30 am. I assured him that there would be hot water available anytime, and that I would be there from 4:30 am onwards.

Lily stayed behind to oversee the group, but I was ready for some much-needed sleep after another long day, knowing that the next day promised to be just as busy. At 4:00 am, I was already awake, the sound of the wind echoing through my tent.

The temperature inside was chilly and I could tell that it would not be a comfortable day outside. As I put on my clothes and shoes, I stepped out to get a better look.

The sky was grey with clouds and the wind was blowing at approximately 20 kilometres per hour. It was clear that it wouldn't be as nice as the day before when we welcomed the group with drinks at the ice bar.

Heading to the kitchen tent, I fired up the gas oven to bake some bread for the day. While it got warm, I took a moment to freshen up by washing my face and brushing my teeth. Next on my list was topping up the five large kettles with water and warming them on the gas stove for coffee and tea. It was an important task to ensure everyone had hot drinks to start their day in such cold conditions.

The bread dough had been left to prove overnight and I shaped it into long thin baguettes. The temperature in the room wasn't suitable for a second proving, so I added extra yeast to the initial mixture. Once the oven reached the desired temperature, I quickly slid the bread inside to minimize heat loss and ensure it cooked at the highest possible temperature. The oven did not have a thermostat, and like many other pieces of equipment (or lack thereof), simple tasks such as baking bread or cooking food were quite challenging and relied heavily on a mixture of luck and skill.

With those first tasks completed, it was time for a cup of coffee. However, I couldn't waste any time as there was an entire breakfast buffet to prepare. I knew from experience that any tasks in Antarctica always took longer than in modern environments due to equipment limitations, reduced space, and numerous distractions throughout the day. Twenty minutes later, my baguettes were perfectly baked and golden brown, sending a tempting aroma wafting through the air. It almost smelt like there was a Parisian bakery next door.

Just as I had taken the bread out of the oven, Raj walked in through the client-side door. It was 5:30 am sharp - his timing was impeccable.

As I washed my hands, I noticed that the kitchen door was slightly open, so, I called out a cheerful *"Hello!"* He suddenly appeared at the doorway and commented on the delicious aroma in the air. *"Good morning, how are you? Did you sleep well?"* I greeted him with a smile.

"Hi Seb, I had a great night's rest, thank you. That smell of fresh bread has made its way to my room - where is it coming from?" he asked curiously.

I pointed to the cooling rack on the table where some freshly baked baguettes were resting and replied, *"It's from our local bakery."*

Raj's face lit up and he exclaimed, *"That's my favourite breakfast treat - the end of a baguette with a bit of salted butter! Could I have some?"*

"Of course, please have a seat in the dining area and I'll bring some out for you," I replied.

"Could I just sit down here at the kitchen table? There are a few questions I'd like to ask you." I nodded and he took a seat with a broad grin across his face.

As we talked, he opened up about his family and business background. He admired the operation and was impressed that it ran so smoothly despite being in Antarctica. While I prepared the breakfast buffet, I rattled off a never-ending list of challenges involved in running such a remote operation. From managing scarce water and food supplies to ensuring that there was enough fuel for our planes, dealing with waste disposal - including the unpleasant task of human waste - and preparing for the unforgiving winter months when everything had to be dismantled and the environment left untouched before our departure. His eyes widened in awe as I went over the immense logistical operation necessary to make this adventure possible, not only for his family but also for the other privileged guests who would join us during the summer season.

After a while, Raj's wife finally arrived and took a seat at the dining table. He expressed his gratitude once more for my knowledge and the tasty baguette and butter, then joined her next door.

Lily arrived too, and began bustling about the kitchen with excitement, preparing all the jams, honey, and juices for breakfast. She carefully arranged them in the dining room on a pristine tablecloth, accompanied by a breadbasket filled with a selection of sliced bread for toast, and some of the fresh baguettes.

Meanwhile, as I had received a bounty of fresh produce the day before with the arrival of our group, and I skilfully utilised it to create a mouth-watering array of food - a rainbow-hued fruit salad, a beautifully arranged charcuterie and cheese board, a decadent platter of smoked salmon, and a creamy bowl of yoghurt, artfully topped with passion fruit and crunchy granola.

But that wasn't all - I had another enticing option for our guests. I had also sautéed wild mushrooms in extra virgin olive oil and delicate baby spinach in a sizzling pan with a touch of garlic. At the same time, I roasted plum tomatoes in the scorching oven, seasoning them with a pinch of sea salt, cracked pepper, and fennel seeds. I delicately plated the ingredients to create a dish that would make anyone's mouth water. I served it alongside some fluffy scrambled eggs and was pleased with the outcome.

The resulting hot breakfast was both simple and delicious, with each bite offering a perfect balance of flavours that danced on the taste buds like a symphony. Raj and his wife both opted for the cooked breakfast with a side of baguette.

Raj kindly asked if he could have fried eggs instead of scrambled, and of course, I happily obliged. As I prepared their food in the kitchen, I couldn't help but overhear their conversation about the challenges of running this place. I smiled to myself at the respect in their voices, happy that they "got" it.

Once their hot food was ready, Lily brought it out to them. More family members started to arrive, adding to the cheerful atmosphere in the dining room. Then, Lily came back to the kitchen and informed me that Raj wanted to speak with me.

Surprised by his request, I made my way over to their table. *"Could you make me some scrambled eggs as well?"* Raj asked.

I was confused, but of course, I responded with a simple *"sure".* He went on to explain that he had tried some of the scrambled eggs I had made for his wife and loved them. He shared that he often ordered scrambled eggs when eating out, but they were usually dry and unappealing.

Curious, he asked for my secret. In response, I shared that it all came down to time - I cooked scrambled eggs like my mentor "Monsieur George" had taught me during my early days as an apprentice chef. He used to work on one of the most luxurious cruise ships of its time, the SS France, and had always emphasised that scrambled eggs are a seemingly simple dish that requires careful attention and patience to perfect.

To make sure they're fluffy, glowing, and delicious requires a slow heating process to prevent overcooking. Once the eggs are slightly undercooked, remove them from the heat source and gently fold in a small chunk of butter. Cover and let them rest, keeping an eye on them to ensure they don't dry out or overcook. Right before serving, add a hint of fresh cream for the perfect finishing touch. *Bon appétit!*

After breakfast, the guides gathered with the group to discuss plans for the day and the rest of the week. The group had decided on two excursions: a visit to a penguin colony and a two-day journey to the South Pole. Unfortunately, the day's weather was less than ideal, but there was hope for improvement the next day.

Shortly after the guests and guides had left for a small hike close to the camp, Luke entered the kitchen to inform me that changes in weather conditions would require the guests to depart for the South Pole after lunch today.

The guides had been reached over the two-way radio and announced the good news to the group, then brought them back for a warm lunch before fitting them with the necessary equipment and clothing. This included issuing them with a sleeping bag rated to -50 degrees so they could spend a nice warm night in the teepees. The good news was that having an uptick in weather forecast was a blessing, especially when it came to making the journey towards the elusive 90° South.

However, it meant that I had to work very quickly and at maximum efficiency. Not only did I have to prepare lunch for the group, but also all the meals for the next two days for everyone on the trip - clients, guides, aviation crew, and doctor included. Luckily, Lily and Elie were there to help without even being asked.

They immediately got to work gathering all the necessary supplies and frantically preparing containers to transport food, organizing cutlery and drinkware, and boiling water for hot beverages. We made sure to include some light, easy-to-eat options such as stews and soups to keep the guests satisfied without feeling uncomfortable. Alongside all that, we prepared gourmet wraps and sandwiches, pies, Mediterranean pasta salad, a variety of fresh fruits, chips and crackers, bread rolls, sweet and savoury muffins, as well as an assortment of candies, lollies, and chocolates. We packed more than enough to ensure that everyone would be well fed. For breakfast at Dixie's camp the next morning after the stopover, we also included some oats that could easily be cooked.

The stopover was necessary for refuelling the plane and allowing the pilots some much-needed rest. The heated main lounge tent was filled with plush chairs covered in fur throws and cushions.

The walls were lined with shelves holding repurposed wooden crates displaying antique skis and petrol lamps. All the vintage equipment gave the atmosphere a sense of nostalgia and adventure.

The teepees had been arranged neatly along the lounge tent, each containing a warm and inviting bed covered in cosy blankets and topped with a hot water bottle for extra warmth.

The gas fireplace in the centre of the lounge had become the gathering spot for fellow travellers to relax and share stories over drinks and a hearty meal. It was clear that every detail had been thoughtfully considered to provide both comfort and a sense of camaraderie for those making the journey towards the South Pole. Less than four hours later, everyone had eaten lunch and packed their gear, ready to board the DC3 plane that would take them on an unforgettable journey. Travelling, working, or visiting Antarctica was heavily dependent on one factor: the weather! No matter how well-trained, equipped, knowledgeable, or skilled you are, the weather can not be controlled. That's why it was common to spend a lot of time waiting for the perfect weather window before taking action, but when it came, it was crucial to take full advantage.

The time while the guests were away, was precious; it allowed us to reset and tidy up everything for their return, plan activities based on the weather forecast, and even grab some downtime if possible.

Two and a half days later, their group returned safely to WFR. Despite the demanding journey on the DC3 and sleeping in a teepee at Dixie's camp, one of the most remote places on Earth, it had been a magical, humbling experience for most of them and they were in good spirits.

After such a long journey, I wanted to make something simple, delicious, and not too heavy for dinner.

The first course consisted of a few delicate bite-sized tarts, filled with caramelised onions and goat cheese, finished off with a touch of fragrant basil pesto.

For the main course, I served a chicken ballotine that had been stuffed with roasted apples and wrapped in crispy bacon. It was accompanied by a lemon and thyme sauce to balance the taste of the dish. To complement the meal, I also prepared tender baby potatoes coated in a zesty salsa verde and a colourful mix of green peas, cherry tomatoes, and courgettes tossed in refreshing mint vinaigrette.

For dessert, my guests were treated to an opulent and visually stunning creation: a mixed red berry Sabayon served with cinnamon ice cream. A French classic delight!

While they had been away, I also had a side project in mind. With there being plenty of blue ice around, I had decided to create dessert bowls entirely out of ice. The process required careful melting to avoid any air bubbles or overheating the water, which would weaken the structure of the bowl. I was a bit apprehensive, but I have to say I really nailed it - the result was stunning!

Using the ice bowls, I placed some marinated berries with a touch of fresh mint, and cinnamon in the bottom. Then, I added a scoop of freshly whipped Sabayon on top and used a blowtorch to caramelize it like a crème brûlée. A small quenelle of cinnamon ice cream completed the dish. Just before serving, I added a little chunk of dry ice and poured over it a snip of warm rum which generated some fog to rise out of the bowl for a dramatic effect.

Elie and Lily burst into the room with a grand flourish, taking the dessert to the dining table. Our guests' eyes widened in awe as they took in the stunning visual display, their mouths watering at the sight before them. It was as if time stood still for a moment as they were completely captivated by the sheer spectacle of it all. It was truly an impressive Antarctic-inspired treat!

As the theatrical and indulgent dessert was served, the guides, along with Luke, joined the group. Conversation flowed effortlessly as they talked about the upcoming weather forecast, their voices mingling with the sounds of clinking silverware and glasses. After much discussion, it was decided that their destination for the next day would be the penguin colony at Atka Bay.

Some members of the group initially seemed hesitant, but it was clear to everyone that their reluctance was only due to exhaustion from a long day. With energy and enthusiasm despite the fatigue, they all agreed to proceed with the plan and confirmed their departure for the next morning after breakfast. Excitement filled the air as they eagerly anticipated their visit to the colony, especially knowing that they could expect to be back in time for dinner.

The next morning, Raj arrived first as usual, albeit a little later than the previous day. He was thrilled about the trip to the South Pole and mentioned that he had slept very well despite being so filled with anticipation for the day ahead. Everyone else also arrived early and during breakfast, their conversations centred around the trip to the South Pole and the stopover at Dixie's. The rest of the group were also looking forward to visiting a penguin colony in its natural environment.

Soon after breakfast, the guides, aviation team, and Docteur Elinor gathered with the guests and without wasting a minute, they were on their way for the short one-and-a-half-hour flight. Luke informed Jason, who was in charge of Atka Bay camp that year, about their estimated time of arrival.

The weather at Atka Bay could be quite different from WFR due to its proximity to the ocean, but on that particular occasion, it appeared to be a nice, sunny day with little wind creating the perfect day for penguin watching. After they landed, the guides expertly navigated through the icy terrain, leading the group to the edge of the colony and reminding them to keep a safe distance from the penguins and their nests, as well as being respectful of their surroundings.

As they approached the colony, the sound of the squawking birds filled their ears. The sight of hundreds of them waddling around on the ice was truly unique and humbling. Some were busy building nests, while others huddled together to protect themselves from the cold. Doctor Elinor began her spiel, educating the spellbound group about these fascinating creatures.

She explained how emperor penguins had adapted to survive in such harsh conditions and how they took turns incubating their eggs while others went out to hunt for food. She also pointed out some of the distinct features of Emperor penguins, like their black and white colouration, which provided camouflage in water.

The guests stood in awe as they beheld the majestic creatures, their sleek black and white feathers resembling a formal tuxedo from a distance. The surprisingly graceful creatures huddled together in groups, seeking warmth and companionship amidst the icy terrain. Others, in single file, waddled around the colony, their movements slow and deliberate as if carefully choreographed. Some penguins stood still for hours on end, while others continued their synchronised march, providing endless opportunities for the fascinated guests to capture the moment through photos and videos.

But as much as they would have no doubt liked to stay forever, eventually, it was time to fly back to WFR. With only two days remaining, Raj and his family were ecstatic. They had achieved their goals and now just wanted to relax and embrace the experience of being in Antarctica.

Like any vacation, people often obsess over capturing the perfect photos and lose sight of living in the moment, but now, they yearned to relax and immerse themselves in each precious second.

The guides arranged for some easy hikes with breathtaking views near the camp, an ideal activity for all ages and levels of motivation. In the afternoon, Raj and his wife came to see me in the kitchen, looking a bit worried.

Before leaving home, they had been unsure about how the catering would work during their holiday, and whether they would enjoy the food that was served. So, as a backup plan, they had brought plenty of

Indian food with them. However, since they loved everything that had been offered, they now had leftover food that they didn't want to take back home.

They asked if I wouldn't mind preparing it for dinner and even insisted on inviting the whole team to join them at the table and share in the meal together. Raj's wife also graciously offered to help me in the kitchen to make things easier for me and suggested making Bloody Marys for everyone as pre-dinner drinks.

It was a fantastic idea and we certainly had plenty of vodka, but unfortunately there was no tomato juice or celery available.

After discussing it with Luke, he informed me that the aviation team from Whichaway was coming over and they had some fresh tomatoes and celery to send with the DC3 later that day. I was happy I would be able to meet Raj's requests, as he had been such a pleasant guest.

Time had gone by so quickly, and now the group's stay was almost over. It felt like just yesterday when Lily and I were frantically setting up the ice bar as Raj and his family were about to land, and now, we were all gathered for a final celebration, sharing drinks and dinner.

The atmosphere was lively, with Raj immersed in conversation with his daughters, his wife preparing the Bloody Marys in the kitchen, and music playing in the lounge. It was almost reminiscent of a New Year's Eve party!

As I turned around, Raj motioned for me to come over. His daughters had noticed a couple of lasagna trays on the stove in the kitchen and wanted to know if they had been meant for dinner that night. I explained that it was what I had originally planned for staff dinner, and Raj suggested we warm it up and add it to the meal for dinner. The girls were thrilled, but I had to admit, combining Italian lasagna with Indian curry was an interesting food fusion - it felt like haute cuisine taken to the next level!

The night stretched into the early hours of the morning, lingering like a most welcome guest. The next day, there were a few groggy heads among the group as we prepared for the imminent arrival of the jet. It also turned out that the departure time had been brought forward due to a sudden change in weather forecast for later in the day. Safety was a top priority, and we didn't want to risk the group getting stranded or delayed. As we said goodbye to our guests, heavy-hearted but filled with fond memories from an incredible week, we exchanged contact details and promised to stay in touch.

They extended an invitation for me to visit them in India, and I couldn't help but wonder if and when our paths would cross again as I watched the jet soar into the sky. I haven't been yet, but only time will tell!

Elie (Dr. Elinor), Lily, and Tash (Dr. Tash) had all proved to be an exceptional team, dedicated to providing our esteemed guests with comfort and satisfaction over the entire season. Their warm smiles and eager hands had made them adept at handling all front-of-house tasks, from serving meals and refreshing drinks to maintaining the luxurious bedrooms and even helping with dishwashing duties.

These capable women had quickly become indispensable, so unmatched was their unwavering commitment and attention to detail. Under their watchful eye, our future guests were sure to feel indulged and well-cared for.

Over the coming weeks and months, we welcomed several groups to WFR. Raj's party was the largest, followed by groups of 4-6 individuals from different parts of the world such as Belgium, France, China, Russia, Switzerland, and the USA.

Interacting with them was a delight and they each brought something unique to the table. However, what united them all was their remarkable humanity and success, combined with genuine humility and strong values. I always looked forward to meeting such extraordinary individuals.

Back to Australia

Returning home was always a challenging experience. Of course, there was the initial excitement of seeing loved ones, reuniting with friends, and returning to familiar places and activities. But as always, the buzz faded quickly.

During my time at the selection centre in Hobart, we had discussed various scenarios, including the topic of returning home after an extended period on ice. Travelling to Antarctica was a special and unforgettable opportunity that only those who had experienced it could truly grasp. We left behind our loved ones and embarked on this once-in-a-lifetime journey having discussed the trip with them in great detail, but even then they could never fully understand the excitement we felt upon our return, just as we couldn't completely comprehend the challenges they faced while we were gone.

It felt as though we had disappeared from their lives for a while, only to suddenly reappear while all along, they had been continuing with their regular routines, often taking on extra responsibilities while we ventured into the vast wilderness. Upon returning to our daily lives, it was important to readjust our expectations and find a balance between work and personal life.

Being aware of this beforehand would help ease our transition back home. I was grateful that we had discussed these topics at the selection centre before leaving, as it made my return much smoother.

We also delved into our motivations for wanting to go to such an isolated location: were we searching for something specific or trying to escape from something? For me, it was always clear that I craved the most remote places...or perhaps I was using them as a form of escape? Honestly, the latter seemed more likely, but fortunately, I had equipped myself with the necessary skills and mindset to confront any challenges upon returning home, which made it easier for me to reintegrate into everyday life after each journey.

I have always had a deep love for international travel, and over the years I've learned to appreciate the journey instead of rushing through it. I enjoyed making stopovers in different locations, taking the time to stretch my legs, savour a good meal, do some shopping, and then continue towards my final destination.

Layovers were no different, and as I strolled through the airport in Singapore, I took the time to look left and right and absorb as much as I could.

As I walked through the terminal, my phone rang; It was a Skype call from my mother in France.

With not much time to spare before boarding my flight to Australia, I answered as I progressed down the moving walkway towards my gate.

Along the way, I noticed an increasing number of people standing to the sides wearing full HAZMAT suits and carrying temperature guns. They seemed to be randomly scanning people and my initial response was confusion. My mother's voice reminded me to be cautious of the coronavirus (later to be known as COVID-19), to which I made a silly comment about there being plenty of Corona beer in Australia.

After spending four months living off-grid, we hadn't been keeping up with international news and I never even got curious about it while I was away.

We were all content living in this idyllic bubble filled with excitement, fun, and adventure, wanting to cling to it for as long as possible.

Reality came crashing down on me abruptly the next day. After arriving in Australia, I went straight to my house and discovered that I had unknowingly been on one of the last international flights to arrive in the country before all international travel was put on hold.

Rumours were circulating in the media about a global travel ban that could potentially last up to two years! It seemed like an unthinkable amount of time for travel to be completely halted. The early stages of COVID-19 were already beginning to bring countless challenges and affect lives worldwide, nationally, and locally.

One of the first things I did was reach out to the market managers I had worked with before my departure to Antarctica. Thankfully, they were happy to hear from me and eager to have me back the following week. However, amidst the relief at having secured my trading positions again, uncertainty began to loom as we were clearly facing not only health concerns but also potential impacts on businesses and economies due to what they were soon to call *the pandemic.*

The lockdowns implemented globally would prove to be one of our biggest challenges in this unprecedented situation.

The impact on tourism was significant, as it was a crucial sector of the Australian economy that we relied heavily upon as stallholders. The second issue arose from the supply chain, resulting in shortages of essential products like flour, oil, and even toilet paper. It was unbelievable to see how quickly people started hoarding it, and even fighting over it, as was shown on the national news. As I watched the chaos unfold, I couldn't help but miss Antarctica and its simplicity. We were now facing a virus causing respiratory infections and mass deaths, yet people were fighting over toilet paper!

That week, I was dealt another blow when the Art & Craft market was cancelled indefinitely.

Soon after, sanitary measures such as social distancing and crowd-gathering restrictions were put in place. Thankfully, the Brisbane City and the Powerhouse were classified as farmers' markets and were allowed to continue trading with strict adherence to social distancing protocols.

Despite all of the restrictions and social distancing measures in place during the pandemic, there were a few silver linings. I found myself living with my two dogs, Paquita and Poppy, in a house on a large plot of land in the Gold Coast hinterland. The slower pace of life allowed me to appreciate my time at home more.

My furry companions and I would frequently explore the outdoors and hike through the surrounding rainforest. Although I still had my two weekly markets on Wednesdays and Saturdays, obtaining essential supplies like flour and oil for the pretzel production became increasingly difficult.

This prompted me to think about alternative sources of income - something that was "COVID proof," as we called it back then.

One evening, as I sorted through my vast collection of photographs from over the years, I reflected on the countless comments I had received from family, friends, and customers about my pictures of Antarctica. Then one day, as I was chatting to the store manager at my local bottle shop, he suggested that I start an online shop selling pictures printed on canvas from Antarctica. This sparked an idea, and with the decline in pretzel sales, I decided I had time to diversify my business.

And so, "Cool Antarctica" was born - a Facebook page where I could sell prints of my stunning photographs from my time spent in Antarctica. As I considered selling prints of my photography, I began researching the market and discovered that there was definitely a demand for unique, visually striking images. This motivated me to delve deeper into my archives and create a curated collection that would be appealing to potential customers.

Luckily, I also found printing companies that offered print-on-demand services with quick turnaround times - perfect for avoiding excessive stock and providing customers with customised options and free delivery. However, selling prints alone would not have sustained a business in such a competitive market. I needed something eye-catching and dynamic.

That's when the idea of selling liquid nitrogen-infused cocktails came to me. While this had been a popular trend in Cape Town, it wasn't as common in Australia at the time.

After researching safety precautions and proper handling techniques, I organised a charity fundraising event for "Guide Dogs Queensland" to offer patrons the opportunity to try these cocktails for a donation of just one "gold coin" – 1 or 2 Australian dollars.

The response to my innovative concept was overwhelmingly positive, and it was time to start experimenting with different cocktail recipes. Both children and adults alike were fascinated by the fog that lifted from the iced cocktails thanks to adding drop of liquid nitrogen added just before serving.

This unique offering gave my business an edge and drew attention. I wanted each drink to have a unique visual element representing Antarctica, which was also reflected in the themed merchandise and pictures I had put together.

The marquee wall featured a stunning frozen landscape as a backdrop, while the banner read,

"NITRO, virgin COCKTAILS.
A cool blast from Antarctica."

I had used the term "virgin" instead of "alcohol-free" to comply with Queensland's license requirements for selling alcohol at markets. I divided my market stall diagonally into two sections to reduce costs and minimise my environmental impact and footprint.

The right side and half of the front counter were dedicated to pretzels, while the left displayed samples of my photographs with information on how to order them. I also sold various products featuring my pictures, such as jigsaw puzzles and Rubik's cubes with different images printed on each side.

Despite the extra effort of transporting more supplies and equipment, the combination of pretzels and cocktails proved to be a hit. My days would start early at the market, selling pretzels to shoppers looking for a quick snack before continuing their shopping. This also allowed me to introduce them to my cocktails for later on, when the sun was shining, and temperatures were rising. As I prepared the drinks, I would often chat with customers about my experiences in Antarctica, incorporating my passion for photography into the conversation.

After much contemplation, I had been able to streamline my stall concept enough that it was manageable by myself, without needing to hire additional help. This kept my overall costs low, which was crucial during the pandemic when fewer people were visiting the market anyway, and any amount of waste could heavily impact profits.

Weeks turned into months, and it became clear that COVID-19 was not going away anytime soon. Emergency health measures forced many businesses to adapt, including driving the now- now-established shift towards remote work for many people. As a result, several of my regular clients disappeared overnight and footfall at the market dropped significantly.

As I sat at my stall one day, gazing out at the empty aisles, I couldn't help but let out a heavy sigh. As the pandemic raged on, its relentless grip tightened around my business, suffocating it just as it had so many others. The once bustling markets were desolate and empty, and restrictions made it nearly impossible to sell anything. After enduring over a year and a half of lockdowns and uncertainty, my income had plummeted by an astonishing 70%, leaving my once thriving business barely clinging to life. The vibrancy that had filled the city had been replaced by an eerie quietness, a haunting reminder of what used to be.

As the end of the year drew near, a heavy feeling settled in my chest. I knew it was time to face the harsh reality - my business was no longer viable.

So, with a heavy heart, I decided to shut its doors in November 2020. Looking back, it was a beautiful journey that had begun with a simple idea I had had while exploring Antarctica. The memories and lessons learned over the years had been priceless, but it was time to move on. The sun shone warmly on my face as I contemplated the journey, a stark contrast to the sadness and finality of the moment. It was as if nature itself was bidding farewell to this chapter in my life. As the days and weeks passed by, I carefully wrapped up each piece of equipment, placing them in boxes labelled with their contents. The process of packing and disposing was disheartening, knowing that these tools had once been my livelihood. But now, it was time for them to find new homes. I donated what I could to friends who would put them to good use, a small consolation for parting ways with my cherished belongings.

As the holiday season approached, I found myself facing a rare opportunity - no work commitments or plans ahead. After years of distractions and responsibilities, I was finally able to fully embrace the Christmas and New Year festivities. It was both daunting and exhilarating, a blank canvas waiting to be painted with new experiences and memories.

A few weeks after my business had closed, I found myself aimlessly scrolling through job listings online. With a hopeful heart, I stumbled upon an intriguing advertisement - a position for a chef at a cafe nestled within one of the most prestigious private schools on the Gold Coast.

Without hesitation, I applied for the job and anxiously waited for a response. To my delight, I received an email informing me that I had been shortlisted for the role. The following week, I walked into the interview room with sweaty palms and a racing heart.

The Executive Chef greeted me, and we chatted about my passion for cooking and experience in managing my own business, as well as my time in Antarctica. As we parted ways, he promised to get back to me within a week. The days dragged on as I eagerly waited for his decision. It felt like an eternity before I finally received an email offering me the coveted position. Filled with excitement and gratitude, I accepted without hesitation. As I settled into my new routine at the cafe, located within the lush green grounds of the private school, it felt stable and secure.

The cafe was bustling with life every day as students, teachers and staff flocked in for their daily caffeine fix, or for delicious snacks and meals. I quickly formed connections with my coworkers - a group of enthusiastic and lively individuals who shared a dedication to excellence and customer satisfaction. We worked together tirelessly to elevate the cafe's menu and ensure our customers were satisfied. But what truly made that job stand out was being surrounded by such spirited, ambitious minds every day. The students, too, showed genuine interest in our food creations and often struck up conversations with us during their breaks or study periods.

It wasn't until Easter of 2022 that life after COVID-19 seemed to have returned to a sense of normalcy. During the school break, I had been sorting through some things in my storage unit when I stumbled upon a few printed pictures from my time exploring Antarctica.

They reminded me of the beauty I had captured through my photography, the fun we had had, and the incredible people I met during my adventures there.

As I sat there, daydreaming about my past travels, it suddenly hit me: I was currently on holiday for Easter, but in a few months, there would be a long school summer break starting in November and lasting until early February, meaning I wouldn't have any work at the cafe!

This realisation filled me with excitement and without hesitation, I messaged Katheryn to inquire if White Desert could use my services once again. A strong pang of intuition filled me, a feeling that after all the struggles, sweat, and misfortune, fate was finally shifting in my favour.

As always, Katheryn's reply came swiftly, but it was a bittersweet one - she was moving on to bigger opportunities in her career. However, she reassured me that she would still be involved with White

Desert until around September and expressed her joy at my wish to return for the upcoming summer season.

As the Easter break came to a close, my heart raced with anticipation and determination as I approached my supervisors. I eagerly explained the rare opportunity to return to Antarctica during the summer hiatus, but that I had every intention of returning afterwards.

To my immense relief and delight, they agreed amicably and showed genuine support for my ambitious intent. With the plans set in motion, I felt exhilarated at the thought of embarking on another journey to that captivating icy land.

But this time, it held an even greater significance - I had a personal goal in mind: to reach the South Pole for my 50th birthday in December. The mere thought of standing at the bottom of the world on such a momentous occasion filled me with overwhelming excitement and unwavering determination.

The last fly out

Between April and July, Katheryn and I had several video calls in the lead-up to the start of the new season, so I knew a bit about the changes she had made to the menus.

The main difference was the new menu which was going to be served on the final day before guests took off from Antarctica for Cape Town.

As always, she had worked wonders and designed a dinner with a "South Pole-inspired" theme. The aim was to link this journey to the South Pole with the first explorers who had braved those icy conditions, using ingredients that resembled the shapes, colours, and textures of the location, while adding a touch of creativity. Once I was on ice, the evening would start with a narrative about how these first pioneers had lived (or rather survived) in the region.

I had already read a lot about the history of Antarctica, and the narrative I settled on went something like this: *The early explorers realised that the hostile climate and terrain of the South Pole would thwart their attempts at a successful mission. Dragging an abundance of supplies in tow, they employed dog sleds to lighten the load, but it still wasn't enough.*

To supplement their dwindling resources, food caches became a necessity. Food was buried deep in the ice and the locations were identified by towering bamboo poles topped with a triangular flag.

Eventually, though, they came across a new kind of sustenance: Pemmican cubes (a blend of dried-out meats, fat, and cereal) and sledging biscuits (a hard biscuit created with flour, butter, baking powder, salt, and warm water) became the primary fuel source for the journey.

These food items were light to carry and did not require any complicated storage or preparation methods. As a rough estimate, these biscuits were ultra-high in calories (6,500 calories for 2 biscuits of 70 grams with 1 50-gram cube of Pemmican), which could mean the difference between life and death.

The human body can succumb quickly to hypothermia if deprived of critical nutrients, but this high-fat, carbohydrate-rich diet enabled the men to push themselves to the brink of their physical limits. I liked to think of these foods as the ancestors of modern-day energy bars; not as tasty, but certainly lifesaving!

I would then kick off the South Pole dining experience by recreating the iconic Antarctic survival meal. I set up an MSR burner in front of the guests and carefully collected ice from nearby, explaining the details the dish they were about to taste and giving them a peek into the rest of the meal.

I kept as much mystery as possible, tormenting their curiosity with mere hints of what was yet to come. The idea was that with every bite, guests would be taken back in time. I placed the metal pot over the MSR burner and waited for the ice to melt and heat up. The air thickened with anticipation as I pulled out a cube of pemmican from my pocket, unwrapped it, and tossed it into the water. With a wooden spoon in hand, I swirled the melted mixture around until it became a Hoosh (the name of the resulting broth). Then, I crumbled two sledging biscuits on top, their dry edges dusting my fingers.

Steam rose from the pot as the smell of Hoosh filled our nostrils. Although not a dish that would have won any culinary awards, its energy-sustaining qualities made it ideal for explorers who needed every calorie they could get. I was often taken aback by how much people usually liked it, though it was likely in part because of the narrative behind it, and because they had also witnessed me create it before their eyes.

The next item on the menu was an "amuse-bouche."

Its purpose was to tease the taste buds and whet their appetite for the main course.

A sardine tin was used as a vessel - tinned sardines having been part of Antarctic exploration since the early 20th century. Firstly, a piece of seared tuna in togarashi spices was placed in the bottom of the tin, followed by a layer of smooth, creamy sardine pâté. Atop this, a drizzle of soy mirin sauce and some pickled ginger to add bite. Finally, the dish was crowned with a dot of kewpie mayonnaise, caviar, and finished with microgreens.

It was a simple yet sophisticated dish that provided guests with a combination of spices, textures, and aromas that created an explosion of flavours on the palate, and an escape from reality to one in which the intrepid explorers of the past roamed this unforgiving land. The amuse-bouche was not only tasty but also visually stunning; its colours reminded us of Antarctica's landscape, surrounded by white glaciers combined with its fiery red sunsets—all encapsulated within one single tin.

The next course was salt and pepper calamari served with a pineapple salsa and a lime dressing.

The calamari were lightly fried in a light tempura batter until golden brown, and seasoned with salt, pepper, and paprika. Accompanying the dish was a fresh pineapple salsa that had been cooked on the griddle until it was lightly charred and had developed an intense sweetness. A squeeze of fresh lime juice added a sharpness to the dish that cut through the richness of the calamari, while a drizzle of olive oil provided an additional layer of taste. For the final touch, the dish was adorned with delicate micro herbs to add a pop of colour and texture. It was then served on a sheet of newspaper on which were several historical articles and facts dating back to the first Antarctic expeditions, adding an extra layer of significance to the meal that further captivated the guests' imaginations as they indulged in this unprecedented combination of ingredients for the very first time. It was not just a delicious course, but a journey through something new and electrifying; all within the heart of Antarctica.

The main course of this incredible night was a succulent beef fillet served on a hot salt slab, with plated creamy carrot and rosemary risotto, pan-fried asparagus, tricolour carrots, and red wine jus.

The beef had been carefully selected and seasoned with herbs and spices to bring out the richness of the meat. It was then cooked on the hot salt slab to seal in the juices, allowing us to enjoy a truly authentic taste despite being in such a remote place in Antarctica.

The beef was accompanied by a bed of creamy risotto that was cooked with fresh rosemary and sweet carrot puree for additional depth of flavour.

The risotto was light yet comforting in its rich texture and savoury seasoning, perfectly complementing the tenderness of the meat. On the side were slivers of asparagus that had been pan-fried in butter until lightly charred and crisp; this provided a welcome crunch and sweetness to balance out the heavier components of the dish. To add vibrancy, baby tricolour carrots were added for texture whilst providing a natural sweetness that lifted the overall plate.

Finally, it was all brought together with a generous drizzle of red wine jus, which added both complexity and sharpness to an otherwise classy dish - creating something extraordinary from something ordinary.

This main course reminded guests not just about Antarctica's wild beauty but also immersed them in an impressive culinary evolution - one that celebrated creativity within every bite.

For dessert, guests had the pleasure of experiencing a unique, white chocolate and Rooibos mousse with cream espuma, vanilla macaron, lychee jelly, and almond crumb.

The mousse itself was light yet full-bodied in its texture and sweetness, with underlying hints of Rooibos that gave it an earthy touch. The espuma provided an extra layer of indulgence with its light and creamy consistency, while the lychee jelly was utterly refreshing.

The crunch of the almond crumb added much-needed texture, completing the dessert perfectly.

The final touch to the dessert was a perfectly cooked macaron made with Madagascar vanilla bean, adding a note of sweetness that tied all the elements of the dish together seamlessly.

Presentation was paramount when it came to this dessert, with the use of a smoke bubble gun making it look like a snow globe inside a glass filled with misty fog. This visually stunning dessert could not have been more perfectly themed and was quite reminiscent of when a blizzard would dissipate and reveal the rugged yet beautiful Antarctic landscape. Similarly, when guests pierced the bubble, they would be able to experience what lay beneath; in this case, a mesmerising dessert combination like no other.

I could see that the dish was inspiring the imaginations of our guests as they admired the intricate details before enjoying each bite—much like one would stand in awe before Antarctica's stunning beauty.

It seemed so straightforward to assemble such meals on paper but putting them together in Antarctica always turned out to be a different matter.

After the menu debrief, I found out that, unlike previous years, I would be moving between multiple sites. The plan was to initiate the Whichaway camp with Ant and after the first guests arrived, he would then fly back to WFR and start work on the nearby Echo camp, a new site which was talked about by White Desert family with extreme enthusiasm.

Echo was indeed an awe-inspiring sight, comprising six futuristic pods resembling spacecrafts that had just landed on a distant planet.

The structures were sleek and modern, with floor-to-ceiling windows that offered sweeping views of the nearby moon-like landscape. The design was distinctly out of this world, and it really did create the feeling of having been transported to a faraway place without ever leaving Earth. I suppose that's the essence of Antarctica! The weather had delayed our departure as it often did, which I welcomed as a chance to get some rest before the summer season. I was very aware of the responsibility awaiting me once we arrived on ice.

As a chef, it didn't matter if there were guests or not, the staff still needed to eat, so it would only be either busy or crazy busy!

The time waiting in Cape Town allowed us to enjoy Mojo market and for me to get hold of some great food that I didn't need to cook myself.

We loved Mojo Market - on a normal day the vast, airy space was filled with an array of vibrant food stalls and lively chatter. The neon signs of the bars beckoned from across the room, and the thumping of fantastic musicians filled the air as we made our way to a booth. We inspected the wide array of cuisines displayed on the menu boards as our mouths all began to water: Italian pasta, Mexican tacos, Hawaiian poke bowls, Japanese sushi, French pastries – and all freshly prepared!

We couldn't resist ordering a plate of Saldanha Bay oysters and mussels that melted in our mouths like butter, instantly reminding us why this was our go-to spot. The pristine waters of Saldanha Bay were the perfect place for oyster farming. The bay benefited from the Benguela current, which was a cold ocean stream coming from Antarctica that flowed north along the west coast of the African continent. As it moved, it carried with it plenty of nutrients, making it a great food source for shellfish in the area. In addition, due to its proximity to the Langebaan Lagoon system, it was warmer than other sections of the Western coast—averaging 13°C in winter and 18°C in summer—making it perfect for oysters.

We spent a week discovering the coastal promenade, scaling Lion's Head and Table Mountain, gorging ourselves on yet more oysters, mussels, and other magnificent bites, accompanied of course by litres of Sauvignon Blanc and pints of South Africa's beloved Castle lager.

All too soon, though, we received word that the weather in Antarctica was clearing up and our journey would re-commence the following morning.

My morning routine had become second nature by then - having taken my last warm shower and packed my bag, I was ready in a tick, reflecting on all the familiar comforts I was about to leave behind - hot showers, flushing toilets, a cosy bed, an unlimited supply of running water, electricity, and the internet. I never really missed them when I was there, but by God did I appreciate them when I was back!

As we made our way to the hotel reception, I could smell fresh coffee brewing downstairs and paused for a moment to take it all in - the sights, the smells, the excitement and anticipation of my fifth journey south. The porters were already lugging heavy bags onto the bus when I arrived.

I was joined by a team of twenty White Desert employees, mainly new hires. Most of them were labourers who would be helping with the establishment of camps - particularly Echo camp, which had yet to be completely finished for its first guests in a few weeks. It only took us 20 minutes to get to the airport in Cape Town, and when we arrived, a few HR representatives were waiting for us. We swiftly went through all the necessary procedures, and soon enough, we were walking down the hallway towards the plane that would take us across the Southern Ocean to WFR.

The flight was smooth, and the onboard meals were divine. I couldn't help but think that it would be fairly easy to become accustomed to this level of luxury travel.

In a few hours, we would arrive at WFR before I would board a DC3 for a speedy 20-minute jaunt over to Whichaway.

To my delight, when I got off the plane, I found Luke waiting for me. He had risen through the ranks while I was away and was now in charge of all operations in Antarctica.

We were both thrilled to catch up on what had happened at the runway and the new Echo camp. Luke showed me the tremendous amount of tradespeople who had been working hard and fast to set up the camp, which needed to be ready for the arrival of the first guests. He then asked if I wouldn't mind staying for a week or two at the runway to assist the chef.

As it was his first time on ice with numerous hungry builders, he told me he could benefit from my experience and know-how as guidance.

The camp was arranged into a complex maze of yellow nylon polar dome tents, approximately 80 of them set up in 10 rows. I rushed to an empty tent and hastily tossed my duffle bag, backpack, and sleeping bag inside before sprinting to the kitchen, a ritual that I had grown used to in this job. No rest for the wicked!

By then, there were almost seventy team members already down on the ice, unpacking all the winterised containers and getting everything ready for the season. Though it was already the start of November, temperatures remained wintry, at -20 degrees Celsius. The wind was still howling fiercely and as the fleeting twilight hours passed, you could feel the temperature dropping even lower.

The unpredictability of the weather made it a challenge to feed the throngs of hungry people. We had only two ovens - a 4-burner gas stove and an ancient 6- burner from a previous company that had existed 20 years prior and was more of a food warmer than an actual oven, so we rotated dishes between the two for efficient timing. Food was defrosted ahead of time to reduce cooking times.

The chefs in Cape Town had done a great job before the season even began by prepping a lot of meals for the camp set-up crowd. Snacks like biltong, Bovril (the meaty cousin of vegemite), and cookies were always available for those who missed meals due to work commitments. Freshly baked bread was constantly being sent out to feed the masses. We were determined not to let anyone go hungry and went to great lengths to make sure we succeeded.

That year, due to the overwhelming number of people, an additional mess tent had been established. This helped a great deal with the kitchen traffic, but we still had to transport food there from the kitchen tent, which was about 30 metres away. It was a difficult task in itself just walking on ice and enduring the temperatures, but when the wind began to blow harshly, our mission felt almost impossible.

Throughout the night, the wind howled with increasing ferocity outside my thin nylon tent. The relentless flapping of the fabric made it impossible for me to sleep soundly.

Although I had earplugs from my airline kit, I was hesitant to use them for fear of missing my alarm. So instead, I tossed and turned throughout the night, only managing to snatch brief moments of shivering sleep. It really was one of the coldest nights I had experienced, and the wind remained powerful and gusty into the morning. I scrambled out of my sleeping bag and somehow managed to squeeze into my pants.

I quickly pulled on a chef's jacket, my Carhartt coat, and my work boots before putting on gloves and sunglasses (Sunglasses were a must in Antarctica, even on hazy days. When the winds blew fiercely, I would wear my ski goggles for extra protection). My beanie was already snugly covering my head from the night; at least that was something extra to guard me against the bitter cold. Fighting against a powerful wind, I could feel the cold seeping through my heavy jacket and gloves as I hurried my way from my tent to the kitchen.

All I wanted to do was switch on the stove and the kitchen oven to get ready to bake some fresh bread. Usually, the rough terrain between my tent and the kitchen wouldn't be an issue; however, that day proved to be different, resulting in a bit of a calamity to say the least!

I stumbled towards the kitchen, buffeted by a powerful gust that threatened to knock me over. Suddenly, I felt a sharp pain in my left knee as I lost my balance, but I managed to remain standing.

When I reached the kitchen tent, I quickly removed my layers and switched on the stove and the oven. I boiled some water and brewed myself a cup of tea before sinking into a chair, drained from the bitter winds between my tent and the kitchen. The warmth of the tent was a welcome relief after facing the relentless gusts outside. As I finished my tea, I decided to bake some bread before carrying on with my daily tasks.

Once that was done, I had to venture out again to reach the shipping container where we kept our backup supplies of dry food. I bundled up in my layers once more before heading out. The containers had been relocated a bit further away that year and it took me a good fifteen minutes to walk there, pulling a sled.

The outbound hike wasn't too bad as the wind was behind me and I had the hoodie of my heavy jacket up, which helped keep me warm even when the winds were at their strongest.

However, the hike back pulling a sled loaded with supplies was another story entirely. The headwinds seemed determined to put an end to my expedition and proved difficult to fight against. The snow lashed against my face and visibility dropped drastically in the blizzard-like conditions. Despite being clad in so many layers, I still felt cold, especially around my nose and cheeks which were already numb from the exposure after just a couple of minutes.

Finally, after what seemed like hours, I made it most of the way back to the kitchen tent safe and sound - or so I thought. Instead, to add insult to injury, I had a second tumble and ended up on the ground. Fortunately, this time, my pride bore the brunt of my damage instead of my body.

After a long day of work and cooking for the masses, I made myself one last cup of tea before heading to my tent for the night.

The wind had died down in the evening, so I was hoping to get a good night's sleep. The next morning, I rolled out of bed feeling stiff and achy. My left knee was swollen and tender to the touch, but I figured it was nothing serious and swallowed some anti-inflammatory tablets. As each day passed, I worked hard to ensure everyone had enough food to eat and the tablets kept me going despite my persistent knee pain.

By the end of the week, the staff members who had joined us for the camp setup phase began to depart for Cape Town.

The following day, I boarded a DC3 plane for a quick 20-minute flight to join the rest of the team at Whichaway. They had already been working tirelessly to ensure everything was in perfect condition for the arrival of our first guests.

As I flew my excitement grew, knowing that the summer season was about to officially begin with the arrival of our visitors. The camp was located on the shores of a freshwater lake in Antarctica's Schirmacher Oasis.

Six state-of-the-art sleeping pods provided visitors with a comfy spot to bed down at night, each containing a writing desk, wash area, and toilet. There was also a sauna with a direct view of the glacier across the camp, the kitchen pod, a shower pod, and three central pods that made up the main living space for guests, comprising the library, lounge, dining room, and a staff quarter.

During the first week, I was fortunate enough to have chef Ant assisting me and Stacey, an experienced White Desert team member, setting up the front of house. They had both done several seasons and would move over to open up Echo camp the following week.

I was grateful for the assistance as it made my job easier and much more enjoyable. Ant was an upbeat individual with a great sense of humour, always ready for a good laugh. The workload was different from the runway, as I needed to focus more on quality and presentation than bulk cooking, and in addition to the clients, I had to prepare food for the staff as well. The team consisted of up to fourteen guests and thirteen staff members.

Villa was our camp manager; Robyn handled front-of-house duties; Lulu and Sasha were the camp attendants; Sergei was the mechanic and chauffeur; Doctor Sean was our medical expert; Manu, Marko, and Matt were the mountain guides; Devon was in charge of maintenance tasks; Gherri was our general hand; Jean Seb was the runway groomer and Picasso wannabe; and I was also a part of the team, of course.

The group hailed from seven different countries with a broad age range and backgrounds. I had worked on multinational teams before and found there was more respect and tolerance, not to mention it being a great opportunity to learn things from one another. It was a miserable day when the first group arrived; bleak, leaden skies and a chilling breeze that blurred any sight of land in the distance.

But this was Antarctica; whatever nature decided to present us with, we would accept it as our destiny. No matter how much one could possibly plan for a voyage down there, there was never a way to entirely predict the hardships of the environment. Suddenly, two vehicles emerged from behind the hills. It was Sergei and Devon, who had driven the first group of guests all the way down from the plateau 12 km away, where the weather was much better.

The pilots of the DC3 plane had safely landed there, dropped off the incoming guests and returned to WFR. From afar, we watched their movements, trying to gain insight into their mood. Even though the conditions were poor, they seemed quite excited – proof that they had gotten used to enduring the elements. As they drew nearer, we greeted them and welcomed them into the warmth and comfort of the camp lounge. It had been a lengthy journey, and it was now time for them to rest before their next move. All hands were on deck to make their arrival as smooth as possible. The guides helped Devon, Serguei, and Gherri move the guests' luggage to their rooms while

Robyn, Sasha, and Lulu welcomed them with a beverage and some words of comfort. Meanwhile, Villa and Dr Sean briefed them about housekeeping, safety protocols, and other important information.

Then, Ant and I got a nasty surprise: some of the food that was supposed to come with the clients had gone missing! We reached out to WFR, but bad weather had moved in, and they weren't able to retrieve it.

Despite our tense situation, we laughed a little and got together to rewrite the menu in case there were any special dietary requirements among the guests.

Finally, after a quick brainstorming session, we headed to the lounge room and introduced ourselves before serving the first meal. Ant asked me whether I wanted to do the presentation or if he should take the lead. I decided it would be better for him to go ahead so I could learn from his expertise in that area. I was an experienced chef, but I had rarely dealt directly with customers.

Observing how he interacted with them was a valuable learning experience that I would carry with me for the rest of my career. When I asked him what his approach was, he simply smiled and replied, "Seb, the key is honesty. We'll let them know about what happened but assure them that we have their stay covered."

Even now, I can recall his calm attitude as he talked to the guests about the recent events and introduced the week's menu in a laid-back manner that put everyone at ease.

As the week came to a close, the departing guests were delighted and praised our team for the quality of cuisine we had managed to provide despite the early setback. That first group's stay went by in a flash, but as we stood there ready to bid them farewell, I could see on their faces that we had not just done a good job, but a fantastic one.

It was also time to bid farewell to Ant and Stacey, who were headed over to WFR to open the majestic Echo camp. As our next group of guests arrived, we were pleased to see that the weather had significantly improved from the previous week's cloudy, windy days, making way for warm, sunny weather with no wind.

On that particular morning, the head guide, Manu, briefed me on the planned activities for the week ahead for our new group of guests. Rock and ice climbing were on the agenda, with assistance from guides Marko and Matt.

Manu also mentioned that they had previously put on a secret picnic on the ice, which had been a massive hit with guests. Of course, it was weather-dependent, but the next day looked like it would be perfect.

The next morning, sure enough, we were greeted by the glorious sunshine and a determination to seize the perfect weather. Robyn, Sasha, and Lulu scurried around gathering all the necessary equipment - plush chairs, cutlery, and luxurious fur covers – as well as organising all the drinks. Meanwhile, I busied myself with preparing an array of delicious cold dishes with delicacies such as prosciutto and charcuterie, succulent hot smoked salmon, delicious French cheeses, sliced fruits, creamy dips, a variety of breads, assorted crackers, and a freshly baked slice of decadent chocolate brownie.

Davon drove us in one of the trucks to our selected location, and we quickly unloaded all of our equipment and provisions. With his help, we set everything up with precision and silence, making sure none of our guests on the other side of the nearby hill would catch on.

As we stood against the massive ice cliff, we took in the breathtaking view of an endless expanse of icy waves blending into the horizon.

With chilled champagne, beer, wine, and whisky at our disposal, we took a moment to relax and enjoy the stunning scenery in front of us, laughing and savouring the moment together as we shared a deep gratitude for this unique experience.

It was a moment of innocence and joy between the five of us. Before long, the group of guests had arrived, accompanied by the guides. The guests were amazed by the sight before them. The guides had skilfully kept the surprise picnic hidden, only mentioning that they would have lunch back at camp. It was a fantastic opportunity for all of us to bond, not only with the guests but as a team, and we promised ourselves to repeat this special experience as often as possible.

And just like that, another week came to an end and a new group arrived. Unlike previous seasons in Antarctica, the weather that year was unpredictable. One week would be perfect, while the next would be the complete opposite. There were even times when the weather was so bad that guests had to stay back for several days because planes from Cape Town were unable to land.

Despite the challenges, though, every moment in Antarctica was one to cherish and remember.

As the days passed, my knee continued to worsen. Doctor Sean kept a watchful eye on me, constantly reminding me to rest and elevate my leg to reduce the inflammation.

However, it wasn't always feasible as I had to be on my feet, cooking for the camp. We tried various treatments, from stronger medication to tightly wrapped compression bandages, but unfortunately, none seemed to be providing any relief.

The pain persisted, and I could feel it intensify with each passing moment, like a ticking time bomb waiting to explode. Eventually, every step I took felt like walking through molten lava, the throbbing ache spreading like wildfire throughout my whole leg. It had become increasingly difficult to conceal my discomfort and push through the daily activities at camp. Something needed to change before it became unbearable.

After weeks of struggling with the pain and swelling in my knee, I finally mustered up the courage to tell Dr Sean that I needed the excess fluid drained.

He gave me a hesitant look and warned me of the potential risks - in that harsh environment, there was no guarantee that my knee would heal properly and if it became infected, I would have had to leave.

It was certainly risky, but I knew deep down that I couldn't continue the season with my knee in such an incapacitated state, so I was willing to take the chance. Dr Sean consulted with Dr Rick at WFR, who made his way over to Whichaway to assist him in performing the procedure.

It was a race against time as we only had a small three-day window without any clients around.

The pressure was on; it was now or never!

When I hobbled into the doctors' pod, it was still in a chaotic state of construction. Being the first patient in what would soon become a state-of-the-art medical area, I couldn't resist leaving my signature on the wall before hopping onto the stretcher.

As I settled in, I felt like a guinea pig under the watchful eyes of the two doctors. But hey, at least I had a fun story to tell at parties! The procedure went smoothly, and both doctors were satisfied with the result. They bandaged my knee to promote blood circulation and prevent further swelling or fluid buildup, and I was instructed to rest and elevate my leg as much as possible for the next three days, while avoiding putting any weight on it.

Devon drove me back to my tent in his truck from the pod. For the next few hours, I struggled to arrange my bags in my tent so that I could lie down comfortably. Since I would be spending the night in a sleeping bag with both legs elevated, this was no easy task.

The doctors left me a two-way radio for communication and provided a pee bottle as I couldn't walk to the toilets on my own. They also arranged for Robyn to bring me dinner later. It was a basic setup in the middle of nowhere, and deep down, I hoped that my knee would heal properly and not get infected.

Despite the awkward position with my legs pointing towards the ceiling of the tent, I managed to sleep fairly well.

However, as I shifted slightly, I realised that I had no feeling in my left leg below the knee. After comparing it to my right leg, I was stunned to find that I couldn't even wiggle my toes on the left foot.

In a state of panic, I quickly unzipped my sleeping bag and inspected it. To my dismay, I saw that it had become swollen; my ankle was now the same size as my calf, and my toes were also significantly larger and completely immobile.

Immediately, I grabbed the two-way radio and called for help. Villa answered with her cheerful voice, and I asked her to contact the doctors and have them come to my tent right away. There was a slight change in her tone, but she reassured me that they had already been notified and were on their way over. Dr. Rick's expression was difficult to miss as he crawled into my tent and saw my injured leg, with Dr. Sean peering in from outside. We exchanged glances, and I couldn't help but think that our risk-taking during the procedure had backfired. However, upon closer examination, Dr. Rick noticed that the bandage had shifted and promptly removed it.

To our relief, my toes began to regain feeling and the swelling in my lower leg lessened. It seemed that spending the night in a sleeping bag had caused the bandage to move. After inspecting my knee, Dr. Rick was satisfied and replaced the bandage, much to the relief of us all.

The weather forecast painted a bleak picture for the day ahead - strong winds up to 80 km/h, poor visibility, and a high chance of whiteout conditions. With safety as the top priority, I was swiftly relocated from my tent to the staff dining pod. The sturdy structure offered shelter from the harsh elements and allowed my colleagues to easily tend to me. From there, Dr. Sean could keep a close watch on my condition.

The howling winds outside seemed muted within the walls of the pod, but their continuous roar served as a constant reminder of the danger that lurked outside. As I huddled inside the warm yet cramped space, I couldn't help but feel grateful for the protection it provided against Mother Nature's fury.

As the days passed, the stormy weather gave way to blue skies and sunshine, allowing Dr. Rick to return to WFR. With Dr. Sean by my side, I began to slowly move around again, mindful of not overexerting myself. Thankfully, the next wave of guests was much smaller in size, which eased the physical strain on my body. I was still extremely cautious, though, making sure that each step and movement was considered in order to avoid any potential aggravation of my injury. It was like walking on a tightrope, balancing between efficiency and pain.

The days passed quickly, and I couldn't believe that it was already time for my next move.

My stint at Whichaway was coming to an end as a new chef was set to arrive, marking my return to WFR for the rest of the season. The mere thought of reuniting with my colleagues and friends at WFR filled me with energy. I was ecstatic when I learned that Ags would also be joining us at WFR as the runway manager for the second half of the season. It felt like a long-awaited reunion with another member of our close-knit family.

Saying goodbye to my fellow campmates was, as always, a bittersweet experience. These strangers-turned-friends had become like family to me in such a short space of time, but now it was time for us to go our separate ways. Though it tugged at my heartstrings, I knew that new adventures awaited me at WFR, and I couldn't wait to see what they had in store.

As I made my way over, the season was coming to an end for Manu and Marko. Stacey and Ant had set up Echo camp and were also preparing for their journey back home with the remaining team members, who had also finished their work. Sergei, our fearless chauffeur, expertly manoeuvred the truck through the rough terrain towards the plateau.

The sun beat down on us as we approached Cody's Twin-Otter plane, which was perfectly polished and glistening in the sunlight, waiting to take us to WFR. Our hearts raced with excitement as Cody performed a daring flyby above the camp and gracefully glided over the glacier. We held our breaths as we navigated through the treacherous fangs of Ulvetanna Peak, feeling both fear and awe at its majestic beauty. And then, with precision and skill, we made a respectful pass over Echo camp before triumphantly soaring toward WFR and landing safely on the runway. It was a moment of pure adrenaline and joy, heightened by Cody's impeccable flying skills.

It was nice to return to WFR - the vast openness of the location, the breathtaking mountain range in the distance, and the lively rhythm of life there all made it such a unique experience. It felt like a constant ballet with planes taking off and landing as guests arrived or departed.

But just as I settled back into the routine, a new situation unfolded rapidly. The chef who had replaced Ant had to urgently return to Cape Town and would be getting off ice with the next plane, which also was bringing new guests to Echo.

Chester (WFR's camp manager) and Luke came to me for advice on what to do. My simple answer was to contact the head office for a suitable replacement, but the reality was much more complicated - I knew it wouldn't be easy to find a chef willing to go to Antarctica at short notice.

To secure some extra time, I offered to take care of the clients at Echo Camp for the next two weeks. After that, there was a two-week gap with no bookings, which would give us a total of a month to find a suitable replacement. Luke and Chester agreed that this was the best solution, and Ags, who had just arrived a few days prior, offered to assist with taking on my responsibilities at WFR. The distance between

WFR and Echo camp was a mere few kilometres, making it easy for me to maintain my tent as my home base.

I commissioned myself a skidoo for transport between the two camps, and the next morning, wrapped in layers of insulated clothing, I embarked on what was a 15- minute journey to Echo. The air was crisp and biting, but the sun shone brightly over the vast expanse of snow-covered land. The roar of the skidoo's engine echoed through the stillness as I navigated through the winter wonderland. Perched atop a small hill, the camp boasted majestic views of Ulvetanna Peak, which could be seen from the floor-to-ceiling windows of the lounge.

The sharp, pointed edges of the peak seemed to pierce the sky and were accentuated by the ice at its base. Ant had thoughtfully set up the kitchen, leaving me with only a few minor tweaks to make before it was ready.

Luckily, I would only have to cater for six guests in the first group and four in the second, making my job much more manageable and allowing me to provide personalised attention to each individual.

Life at Echo was made infinitely easier by the presence of a few well-connected acquaintances. Graham, a stalwart figure in charge of maintenance and a key player in constructing the camp from the ground up, exuded an air of profound knowledge about the place.

His seasoned wisdom and strategic insights proved invaluable time and time again. One such suggestion was to create a food storage space in the blue ice down below. The idea immediately sparked my interest, and I could already envision the practicality of it.

Without wasting any time, Graham set to work with his trusty shovel, digging a 3x3 metre hole five metres deep into the blue ice by hand. As if that weren't impressive enough, he also cleverly carved out a set of stairs leading down into the ice cave. It truly was a marvel to behold as it kept the food at a constant -20°C and, most importantly, it was sheltered from the elements, especially the sun. I couldn't help but admire his resourcefulness and determination as he continued to shape and mould the space into a functional food storage unit.

Dave, our resident doctor at Echo, was not only a skilled medical professional, but also an invaluable member of the team on a personal level. His infectious energy and joyful attitude radiated positivity wherever he went. Always eager to lend a helping hand, I tasked him with creating some pre-dinner canapes one afternoon. With creative freedom in mind, he quickly got to work, surveying the ingredients available to him. After careful consideration, he presented us with a stunning dish: "Bloody Mary & Oyster Shooter with Horseradish and Caviar." The unique creation consisted of a shot glass filled with the classic Bloody Mary cocktail, topped with a plump oyster resting on the glass in its shell, with a small stick of fresh celery, a hint of horseradish, and a touch of caviar on top.

As our guests eagerly devoured the elegant and succulent treats, it was clear that Dr. Dave's culinary skills were just as impressive as his medical expertise. Working at Echo during the day and riding back on a skidoo at night provided a sense of routine, almost as if I was commuting home from work. Plus, with fewer clients, I saw this as an opportunity to achieve one of my dreams for the season: visiting the South Pole on my 50th birthday.

One evening, as I returned to camp, Luke was still there, and we caught up on how things were going at Echo. I took the opportunity to ask him if there would be a chance for me to join the trip to the South Pole, given the low number of guests.

However, his response lacked the enthusiasm and optimism I had hoped for. Disappointment settled in as I realised that my dream may well not become a reality. But deep down, I understood and respected his decision as the team leader. On changeover day, our group of six guests waited for pickup while another group of four arrived. In the distance, I could see a vehicle driving swiftly through the snow mist towards Echo.

From its driving style, I knew it was Luke behind the wheel doing the changeover. As the vehicle came to a stop in front of camp, we said goodbye to the departing group and welcomed the new arrivals.

It was indeed Luke and as he stepped out, he saw me, waved me over, and announced that he had secured a spot for me on the plane that was taking the new guests to the South Pole in a couple of days.

The news echoed in my ears, and I felt a mixture of disbelief and excitement swirling inside me. I couldn't believe that I was finally going to make it to the South Pole - and on my 50th birthday! It was a dream I had cherished for so long, and it was now becoming a reality. Luke's face beamed with joy as he watched my reaction. *"I know how much this means to you,"* he said, patting me on the back. *"We've managed to squeeze you on the plane - make sure it's an unforgettable experience."* Tears welled up in my eyes as gratitude overwhelmed me.

The next few days were filled with anticipation that gripped me tightly. The camp hummed with excitement as preparations were made for the journey. My mind raced with thoughts of what lay ahead - the extraordinary beauty and solitude that awaited me not only at the South Pole but also during our overnight stay at Dixie's. Eventually, the day arrived.

The plane stood before us, its propellers whirring as if the vessel itself was eager to embark on this remarkable adventure. I joined the small group of guests, their faces mirroring the same mixture of excitement and wonder. As we boarded the plane, I took a deep breath and tried to calm my racing heart.

As soon as the engine roared to life, any lingering doubts or fears were drowned out and with each passing moment, we soared higher into the vast expanse of blue sky and endless ice below us in every direction. It was incredible. Hours turned into an eternity as we flew over the frozen landscape until, finally, the long-awaited call from the pilot came - we were about to land at the South Pole. I gazed out the window beside me and was met with a breathtaking view of the icy terrain below.

After a while, the pilot's voice crackled over the intercom, announcing our arrival. *"Welcome to the South Pole,"* he said. *"Prepare for landing."*

The plane touched down on the snow-covered runway, and a wave of emotions washed over me. I couldn't believe that I was finally there, at the southernmost point on Earth. The magnitude of the moment was quite overwhelming. Stepping off the plane, I was immediately greeted by a blast of freezing cold air that seemed to cut through every layer of clothing. The bite reminded me of the harshness and rawness of that untouched wilderness, and I found myself almost subconsciously pulling my Carhartt jacket tighter around my body.

The sky was clear, but the wind was blowing at about 30km/h, adding a great level of wind chill to the -20°C outside temperature, making it feel more like -35°C. The elevation at the South Pole was about 2,700 metres above sea level. I couldn't help but feel a profound sense of awe as I took in the stark beauty of the icy landscape stretched out before me, seemingly endless in its vastness.

The air was thin and crisp, forcing each breath to be deliberate and measured, and the wind howled relentlessly, tugging at my clothing and chilling me to the bone.

As we moved further away from the plane, I caught sight of the Amundsen-Scott South Pole Station, a research station run by the United States. Its name paid homage to Roald Amundsen of Norway and Robert F. Scott of Britain, both of whom had led expeditions in 1911/12 to become the first to reach the South Pole. I joined the four guests as we made our way towards the Ceremonial and Geographic Poles. The striped pole with its mirrored ball shimmered under the sunlight, a beacon amidst the frozen wilderness. It was a symbolic reminder of human achievement and exploration in one of the most inhospitable places on Earth. As we neared the marker, I couldn't help but reflect on the extraordinary journey that had brought me there.

From my humble beginnings in Marlenheim, France to this monumental landmark on Earth, it was a testament to my own perseverance and the power of dreams. We huddled together at the poles, bundled up in our warmest gear, as our guide regaled us with tales of those who had gone before us. Stories of daring explorers like Scott and Amundsen resonated in my mind, their bold expeditions etched into history as my own trips would be forever etched into my memory.

After an hour had passed, we got on the plane to begin our journey back. We would be stopping at Dixie's camp for the night, just a short two-hour flight away. Luke's unexpected gesture had made it all possible, and I knew I would never forget his kindness. I couldn't wait - I had secretly packed a bottle of whisky and some food for my friends Pasha, Dimitri, and Andrei. They had no idea I was on the plane. As we arrived, the three of them were completely surprised; they hadn't been expecting me, let alone whisky!

I made my way with the guests to the lounge where Pasha had already prepared a beef Bourguignon for dinner. The tent was warm and cosy, with a humble yet charming atmosphere. We all ate together quietly as the tiredness began to set in. The warmth from the heater only added to our exhaustion. Some of us sat on chairs, others on recycled crates, while some stood - a nice change after hours of sitting on the plane. We reflected on our journey so far as we enjoyed our meals and drinks.

The evening didn't last long, as most of us were eager to get some rest after being awake for over 24 hours. Before heading to my teepee, though, I decided to catch up with my friends. As I walked across the ice towards their quarters a few hundred metres away, I realised that sleep would perhaps have been a better idea.

But when I saw them, all three welcomed me with open arms and insisted that we share a drink. Of course, it quickly turned into more than just one. The layover proved to be an unexpectedly delightful experience for the guests, offering a true sense of Antarctica's vastness, especially when we were standing in front of the sign proclaiming our nearest neighbour to be the International Space Station (ISS) 400km above us!

We spent a wonderful evening catching up on everything that had happened during the season and shared both our triumphs and challenges. The atmosphere was joyful, and we had a great time well into the early hours of the next day.

As I headed to the guest lounge to prepare breakfast and brew some coffee and tea for when people woke up, I realised I had left my Carhartt jacket at my friend's quarters. I quickly made my way back to retrieve it. Upon arriving, Andrei warmly welcomed me back and insisted I take a seat as he poured us some more whisky.

He then declared that this would be a day I'd never forget. And he was right - I will always remember it, though perhaps not for the reasons he had originally envisaged.

First, he offered to cook me breakfast and suggested an omelette, to which I happily agreed, not being picky about food. He placed a frying pan on the stove and began chopping onions, tomatoes, and bacon on a large cutting board with a chef's knife.

As the drinks flowed and the atmosphere grew more jubilant, I found myself laughing more than I had in a long time. Dimitri attempted to engage me in conversation, but the whisky seemed to have got the better of him, and he stumbled and fell to the floor.

While Pasha went over to help him up, I watched Andrei continue his cooking preparation. But then, out of the blue, he accidentally chopped off part of his thumb!

The situation was getting out of hand, but thankfully Pasha quickly jumped in again to assist Andrei and stop the bleeding before bandaging his wound.

Despite the chaos, Andrei insisted on finishing making the omelette, and after some commotion, we finally sat down to eat.

As I moved my fork through the eggs, I noticed what looked like a piece of Andrei's missing finger. Without causing any fuss, I simply set it aside and finished my meal. By this point, all inhibitions were gone thanks to the amount of whisky we had guzzled.

The four of us had a last send-off toast and I grabbed my Carhartt to make my way towards the plane as I heard the guests starting to move in that direction too.

The last stretch of the flight was smooth and enjoyable, allowing everyone to take in the breathtaking views of the Antarctic scenery. As I gazed out at the endless expanse of ice and snow, a sense of tranquillity washed over me. The world and its problems seemed distant and insignificant compared to the grandeur of this frozen landscape. In this remote wilderness, I felt connected to something greater.

We landed back at WFR with a group of pleasantly exhausted passengers who had just experienced a once-in-a-lifetime trip to the South Pole.

After our four guests departed from Echo, there were no clients booked for the next two weeks. I went back to WFR to take over from Ags and the volunteers who had been filling in for me. They had done a fantastic job, according to the feedback I received. Kudos to Ags.

As I returned, Chester, Luke and I chatted about the approaching end of the season. It was almost time for many at WFR to pack up and leave over the next few weeks as the season came to a close.

I suggested a surprise Braai (BBQ) for everyone to enjoy, but not at the runway; instead, I had found a nice spot during my trips between Echo and WFR.

My idea was met with enthusiasm and Chester helped me load all the necessary equipment, the BBQ, and plenty food onto two sleds, which we then towed with our skidoo to a beautiful lookout over the distant mountain range. It was out of sight from camp but not too far away. As we made our way towards our chosen spot for lunch, I couldn't contain my excitement.

I quickly got to work setting up the BBQ, cooling down drinks, arranging the main table, and preparing plates, condiments, and snacks while Chester went back to camp to gather the rest of the team.

At 1:00 pm, he returned with everyone eagerly seated on either a sled, skidoo, or truck, ready for lunch. They were all curious about what was happening and when Chester announced that we were having an afternoon off, cheers erupted from all directions.

Standing there surrounded by untouched snow and endless white landscapes, I couldn't help but feel happy for this moment of peace leading up to the end of a busy and eventful season.

With the BBQ now fully stocked, my friend Louis offered to take on the important role of Braaimaster. He would be in charge of grilling our selection of meats, which I had carefully chosen to recreate a traditional South African braai experience. We had marinated chicken, lamb chops, boerewors (a type of sausage), rib-eye steaks, and even snoek (a type of fish). But the most important item was the beloved braaibroodjie (grilled cheese sandwich).

Braaibroodjie are the highlight of many a braai. In between two slices of bread you'll find chutney, onion, tomato, cheese, salt, and pepper as filling. The bread is then buttered on the outsides and cooked on the braai.

The smell of sizzling meat filled the air as we joked and laughed together. During lunch, I took a moment to look around at my colleagues, some of whom had become good friends over our time working for White Desert. Each person had their own unique stories and backgrounds, but there, in that remote place, we had all come together to work towards a common goal: Making sure that each guest has an outstanding experience in Antarctica.

It was moments like these that made me appreciate our tight- knit community even more. The party was blessed with perfect weather, the sky was clear blue and there wasn't even a hint of wind. We spent the entire afternoon on the hill, soaking up the beauty around us. Certain moments are like rare gems, too precious to be recreated or bought with all the money in the world.

As the end of the season neared, Luke informed me that Stacey would be returning to assist with packing up Echo and conducting a thorough inventory check.

I was delighted to have her back and relieved to get a bit of help, as the task seemed daunting. She arrived a few days later and quickly got to work organizing all of Echo's gear and supplies. With her assistance, we were able to finish the inventory check in just a few days, but as we went through each item, I couldn't shake off a sense of sadness.

WFR had been my home away from home for the past several months. I walked through the now-desolate campsite, a melancholic feeling lingered in the air - a mix of nostalgia for the summer that had come to an end, and anticipation for what the future held.

The energy was palpable as everyone hurried to complete their tasks before the last fly-out. People scurried about in all directions, desperately trying to pack up and secure everything before the deadline arrived. The once lively and bustling camp now resembled a deserted colony, with tents and equipment carefully disassembled and stored away. In the distance, vehicles were being prepped and winterised, ready to brave the impending snow and ice.

My friend Lukas, the master mechanic of our team, diligently tended to the upkeep of our fleet. With meticulous care, he inspected and replenished the engine oil, hydraulic oil, coolant, and JetA1 fuel, leaving no room for error. Each vehicle was treated like a prized possession, ready to take on any challenge that might come its way. After the servicing was complete, he would take extra steps to ensure the vehicles were protected during the harsh winter season. He strategically placed them on raised snow berms, reaching heights of approximately 5m, which prevented any snow buildup. This precaution meant we wouldn't have to dig the vehicles out from under mounds of snow a few months down the line. Not satisfied with taking just basic precautions in the Antarctic winter conditions, Lukas also went above and beyond by covering all open pipes and vents with specialized materials. Air intakes, exhausts, cab breathers, window seals, and door frame gaps were all meticulously sealed off to prevent any stray bits of snow or ice from entering critical areas of the vehicles, like the engine and the driver's cab. Then, as a final measure of protection, he disconnected the batteries to prevent them from draining. With such thorough preparation in place, we were able to rest assured that when we needed our vehicles the following season, they would be in tip-top condition and ready for whatever lay ahead.

From a bird's eye view, it would have appeared as a hectic yet perfectly coordinated ballet, reminiscent of a bustling colony of ants preparing for hibernation. Each individual tirelessly worked towards the common goal of preparing for the long winter ahead.

Finally, we caught sight of our plane in the distance. It was an intense moment as we had just finished packing up our entire base camp, which had provided us shelter and warmth against the harsh Antarctic weather. Together, we had endured storms and setbacks, but it was now time to say goodbye.

I took a deep breath as I boarded the plane and settled into my seat by the window, marvelling at the mountain range in the distance. It never failed to amaze me!

As we taxied towards the end of the runway, I reflected on all the friendships I had made over the years and the incredible people I had met. They would stay in my memories forever.

With a sudden roar, the powerful engine jolted to life, propelling us forward with incredible force. The deafening sound filled the cabin, and I could feel the vibrations of the icy runway beneath the wheels of the plane. In an instant, we lifted off and soared into the sky. As we ascended, the cabin became quieter, and the only sounds that remained were the hum of the engine and the gentle whir of the air vents. My ears popped briefly as we turned north, leaving behind the frozen landscape and passing by the majestic Ulvetanna Peak.

I stared out the window, looking down at the awe-inspiring landscape that I was leaving behind me for the last time, I reminisced about every challenge I had faced during this once-in-a-lifetime opportunity and the strength, commitment, and optimism it had taken me to overcome it all.

As I became lost in my thoughts, a line from one of the bravest Antarctic explorers came to mind:

"Difficulties are just things to overcome after all".
(Ernest Shackelton 15th December 1900)

Epilogue

The gruelling 2022/23 season had put both my physical and emotional strength to the ultimate test. For close to 100 long, arduous days, I had persevered through excruciating pain due to the injury to my knee and my sore back, all while surviving in a cramped, flimsy nylon tent atop the icy terrain.

Every day was a battle, a constant struggle against the elements, but I refused to give up. The unforgiving cold pierced through every layer of clothing, while the never-ending expanse of white ice and snow seemed to mock my efforts.

Yet, I persisted, driven by a fierce determination to overcome the challenge and emerge victorious. It was a true test of resilience, one that pushed me beyond my limits, both physically and mentally.

But in the end, I emerged stronger than ever before, ready to conquer whatever obstacles life might throw my way.

With every fibre of my being exhausted and drained, I made the gut-wrenching decision that this was my last trip to Antarctica.

The harsh landscape and treacherous conditions had taken their toll, leaving me feeling quite broken and hollow.

Then, just as I returned to Australia, my heart shattered once more with the news of my partner's mother, Carole, passing away.

It was a tragic event that forced me to confront my own mortality and reassess my priorities. It was that moment that truly reinforced the decision that I could never again subject myself to the unforgiving grip of the South.

As I reflect on my expeditions to the icy landscape of Antarctica, I am filled with a sense of awe and gratitude. The memories made and bonds formed with remarkable individuals will forever hold a special place in my heart.

Yet, as I turn towards a new chapter in my life, I can't help but feel excited to pursue my passion for cooking and to cherish every precious moment with those who mean everything to me.

The future is bright and full of exciting possibilities. And, as I always say:

Never Give Up on Your Dreams!

In loving memory of Carole.